THE SONG OF THE HORSE

THE SONG OF THE HORSE

A Selection of Poems
1958–2008

Samuel Hazo

Autumn House
Press

PITTSBURGH

Autumn House Press Staff
Executive Editor and Founder: Michael Simms
Executive Director: Richard St. John
Community Outreach Director: Michael Wurster
Co-Director: Eva-Maria Simms
Fiction Editor: Sharon Dilworth
Special Projects Coordinator: Joshua Storey
Associate Editors: Anna Catone, Laurie Mansell Reich
Assistant Editor: Courtney Lang
Editorial Consultant: Ziggy Edwards
Media Consultant: Jan Beatty
Tech Crew Chief: Michael Milberger
Administrator: Rebecca Clever
Volunteer: Jamie Phillips
Intern: Bernadette James

ISBN: 978-1-932870-21-3
Library of Congress Control Number: 2007943443

For Mary Anne,
our son Samuel Robert and his wife Dawn,
and our three grandchildren—
Samuel Anthony, Anna Catherine, Sarah Grace,
and in memory of my brother,
Robert George Hazo

CONTENTS

ACKNOWLEDGMENTS

Grateful acknowledgment is made to the editors and publishers of the following journals, magazines or books in which some of the poems in this volume first appeared: *The American Scholar, Antaeus, Antioch Review, Arts and Letters, Atlantic Monthly, Beloit Poetry Journal, Carolina Quarterly, Cedar Rock, Chicago Choice, Commonweal, Critic, Crosscurrents, Dickinson Review, Four Quarters, Georgia Review, Greenfield Review, Harper's, Hawaii Pacific Review, Hollins Critic, Hudson Review, Image, Janus Head, Kansas City Review, Kenyon Review, Malahat Review, Mediterranean Review, Mid-Century American Poetry Review, Michigan Poetry Review, Minnesota Review, Mississippi Review, Mystique, New Directions in Prose and Poetry 41, New Letters, New Orleans Review, New York Times, Notre Dame Review, Notre Dame Magazine, Ontario Review, Organica, Painted Bird, Pittsburgh Post-Gazette, Poetry Miscellany, Prairie Schooner, Sagatrieb, Salmagundi, Samizdat, Saturday Review, September 11, 2001: American Writers Respond, Sewanee Review, Shenandoah, Southern Review, Stand, Tar River Poetry, Texas Observer, Texas Quarterly, Transatlantic Review, Virginia Quarterly Review, Water Stone, Worcester Review, Yale Review.*

Special thanks to the University of Arkansas Press for permission to reprint poems that first appeared in *The Past Won't Stay Behind You, The Holy Surprise of Right Now,* and *As They Sail.*

The first section of the "At the Site of the Memorial" is engraved at the entrance to the park in Harrisburg, Pennsylvania, that honors those Pennsylvanians awarded the Congressional Medal of Honor from the Civil War to the present.

PREFACE TO A POETRY READING

Since eyes are deaf, and ears are blind to words
in all their ways, I speak the sounds I write,
hoping you see what somehow stays unheard
and hear what never is quite clear at sight.

CAROL OF A FATHER

He runs ahead to ford a flood of leaves—
he suddenly a forager and I
the lagging child content to stay behind
and watch the gold upheavals at the curb
submerge his surging ankles and subside.

A word could leash him back or make him turn
and ask me with his eyes if he should stop.
One word, and he would be a son again
and I a father sentenced to correct
a boy's caprice to shuffle in the drifts.

Ignoring fatherhood, I look away
and let him roam in his Octobering
to mint the memory of those few falls
when a boy can wade the quiet avenues
alone, and the sound of leaves solves everything.

GOD AND MAN

After casting the first act, checking sections
of scenery and mastering His rage
because the female lead blundered on page
one, He left the actors to themselves on stage
without a script and fretting for directions.

The tongue of the bell must bang
  the bell's cold shell
  aloud to make the bell
  a bell.
        No otherwise exists.
What else is every iron
  peartop but an iron
  peartop if it simply cups
  its centered stamen still?
The frozen pendulum strikes
  nil.
     It plumblines
down like double hands
  made one at half past six.
I've seen the carilloning
  tulips battened down
  in belfries.
        I've heard them
rock and creak in rainy
winds.
        I've felt the dangled
nubs inch close to sound
but never close enough
before the muting night
enshrines them in their brass
monotony.
        It takes the tugging
down and easing up
on one low-knotted rope
to jell the shape and sound
of what remembers to become
a bell.
        And gong after gong
it goes, it goes, it goes....

And tones go sheeping over,
  after, under one
  another, shuddering in high
  cascades from quick to quiet.
The muffled bellbeat
  in my chest rhymes every
  beat of the bell with breath.
It tolls my seven circles
  in the sun.
           It thunders in my
wrists.
        It does not rest.

Each poem I surprise from hiding
  is a face I learn to draw
  by drawing it.
            Masterplan?
None.
      Strategy?
               None except
  whatever wits I pit
  against myself to bring it
  off.
      Never the face
  imagined nor a face in fact,
  my making is its own solution.
It tells me how it must
  become, and I obey or else.
I see myself as some
  lost swimmer of the night
  who must discover where
  he goes by going.
            Uncertain,
  dared and curious, I stall
  my dive until the surface
  stills its saucered ditto
  of the moon.
           Then, plunge....
Sleep's inland waves lock over
  me.
      Ashore, the sea level
  world of pistols, pork chops,
  mirrors and garbage ripens
  into headlines.
           But where I
  plummet, horses ride on wings,

water burns, and willows
write their reasons in the wind.
The pure imagination of a dream
 is mine to swim until
 the baiting light betrays
 me.
     And I rise.
                The shore
 steadies where I left it.
                    The whole
 unfloatable and failing world
 goes by as given.
                I swim
 from maybe to the merely real
 and make them one with words.
I wonder how I did
 it.
     I wondered how I'll do
 it.
     And I've done it.

Coax it, clutch it, kick it
  in the gas was every dawn's
scenario.
              Then off it bucked,
backfiring down the block to show
it minded.
              Each fender gleamed
a different hue of blue.
Each hubcap chose
  its hill to spin freewheeling
into traffic.
              I fretted like a spouse
through chills and overboiling,
jacked my weekly flats
and stuffed the spavined seats
with rags.
              Leaking, the radiator
healed with swigs of Rinso,
brake fluid and rainwater.
                            Simonized,
the hood stuck out like a tramp
in a tux.
              All trips were dares.
Journeys were sagas.
                      From Norfolk
to New York and back,
I burned eleven quarts
of oil, seven fuses
and the horn.
                  One headlight
dimmed with cataracts.
                          The other

funneled me one-eyed
through darker darks than darkness...
O my Roosevelt coupé, my first,
. my Chevrolet of many scars
and heart attacks, where are you
now?
      Manhandled, you'd refuse
to budge.
        Stick-shifted
into low, you'd enigmatically
reverse.
      Sold finally
for scrap, you waited on your treads
while I pocketed thirty
pieces of unsilver and slunk
away—Wild Buck Hazo
abandoning his first and favorite
mount, unwilling to malinger
long enough to hear
the bullet he could never fire.

Down on my knees and palms
  beside my son, I rediscover
  doormats, rugnaps,
  rockerbows and walljoints
  looming into stratospheres
  of ceiling.
           A telephone
  rings us apart.
              I'm plucked
  by God's hooks up
  from Scylla through an open door,
  Charybdis in a socket and a Cyclops
  lamp that glares floorlevel
  souls away from too much
  light to lesser darknesses
What god in what machine
  shall pluck my son?
             Amid
  the Carthage of his toys, he waits
  unplucked, unpluckable.
                I
  gulliver my way around
  his hands and leave him stalled
  before the Matterhorn of one
  of seven stairs.
           Floorbound,
  he follows, finds and binds
  my knees with tendrils of receiver
  cord.
         I'm suddenly Laocoon
  at bay, condemned to hear
  some telephoning Trojan offer
  me a more prudential life
  where I can wake insured

against disaster, sickness, age
and sundry acts of Genghis
God.
        Meanwhile, I'm slipping
tentacles and watching my
confounding namesake toddle free....
Bloodbeats apart, he shares
with me the uninsurable air.
We breathe it into odysseys
where everyone has worlds to cross
and anything can happen.
Like some blind prophet
cursed with truth, I wish
my son his round of stumbles
to define his rise.
        Nothing
but opposites can ground him
to the lowest heights where men
go, Lilliputian but redeemable.
Before or after Abraham,
what is the resurrection and the life
except a father's word
remembered in his son?
        What more
is Isaac or the Lord?
        Breath
and breathgiver are one, and both
are always now as long
as flesh remembers.
        No
testament but that lives on.
The torch of blood is anyone's
to carry.
        I say so as my son's
father, my father's son.

My boys, we lied to you.
The world by definition stinks
of Cain, no matter what
your teachers told you. Heroes
and the fools of God may rise
like accidental green
on gray saharas, but the sand
stays smotheringly near.

Deny me if you can. Already
you are turning into personnel,
manpower, figures on a list
of earners, voters, prayers,
soldiers, payers, sums
of population tamed with forms:
last name, middle name, first name—
telephone—date of birth—

home address—age—hobbies—
experience. Tell them the truth.
Your name is Legion. You
are aged a million. Tell
them that. Say you breathe
between appointments: first day,
last day. The rest is no
one's business. Boys, the time

is prime for prophecy.
Books break down their bookends.
Paintings burst their frames.
The world is more than reason's
peanut. Homer sang it real,
Goya painted it, and Shakespeare
staged it for the pelting rinds
of every groundling of the Globe.

Wake up! Tonight the lions
hunt in Kenya. They
can eat a man. Rockets
are spearing through the sky.
They can blast a man to nothing.
Rumors prowl like rebellions.
They can knife a man. No one
survives for long, my boys.

Flesh is always in season:
lusted after, gunned, grenaded,
tabulated through machines,
incinerated, beaten to applause,
anesthetized, autopsied, mourned.
The blood of Troy beats on
in Goya's paintings and the truce
of Lear. Reason yourselves

to that, my buckaroos,
before you rage for God,
country and siss-boom-bah!
You won't, of course. Your schooling
left you trained to serve
like cocksure Paul before
God's lightning smashed
him from his saddle. So—

I wish you what I wish
myself: hard questions
and the nights to answer them,
the grace of disappointment
and the right to seem the fool
for justice. That's enough.
Cowards might ask for more.
Heroes have died for less.

SPLITTING

Unchanged, my whiskersnow of salt
  and pepper in the sink, the shaver
  shearing my chill cheek war,
  a palmweight of buzzering.
                         With half
  my face to do, a higher power
  sizzles my razor mute.
                Only
  my passport knows me now.
My mirror shows me half-American,
  half-Adam....
                Beyond my balcony
  all Zurich rises to a signature
  of skyline.
           Half here, half home,
  half shaven, half asleep, I could be
  watching Cairo, Istanbul, Madrid,
  Beirut.
         A pigeon waves goodbye
  with both its wings and swerves
  for France.
           My western stare
  outflies it to the Spanish coast,
  the sea and, all at once,
  the States, the States!
              What is it
  to be gone but never gone?
What leaves me more American
  in Zurich than in Pennsylvania?
For answers I might interview
  those voyagers who've docked with God
  or be myself in different
  hemispheres at once.

The Tartars
understood.
Away from home,
they kept their jackboots double-soled
with China's soil—so, no matter
where they walked, they walked on China.

A white stern-wheeler slides
  downriver for Ohio.
                Its paddles
  plow the river rough until
  they seem to falter and reverse.
I've seen the same illusion
  in the backward-spinning tires
  of a car accelerating forward,
  props revolving clockwise
  counterclockwise, trains departing
  from a town departing from a train
  departing.
          To break the spell,
  I focus on the stern-wheel's hub
  and slide into a memory of Paris....
At Notre Dame a life
  I seemed to know preceded me.
On Montparnasse I told myself
  I must have come that way
  before I came that way.
No matter where I walked,
  I kept retreating into what
  came next.
          Even the Seine
  deceived me with its waves blown
  west, its current coasting east....
The wheel I watch keeps wheeling
  me behind, ahead, around.
I clutch my lashes to the wind
  and wait.
         When I release,
I know a place I've never seen.

I see a time I've known
  forever.
       Is it tomorrow, yesterday,
  today?
       I drink a breath.
I breathe my life away.

Your shores diminish.
              You learn
   the doom of sailors drifting
   south on ice islands.
What echoes shall you code
   to float the sea?
              When Manolete
   got it from Islero in Linares,
   he rose again as four
   stone matadors in Córdoba.
Likewise Philippe-Auguste,
   who paid his bodyguards with whores
   to keep them loyal.
              This side
   of memory, you fight the killing
   tides to death for etchings
   on a rock, for life.
              As for
   the Happy Isles?
              Let dreamers
   dock there.
              Believe in such,
   and you'll believe that Essex,
   More and Mary of Scotland
   kidded the chopper on their climb
   to God.
              Settle for the whirlpool
   and the cliff.
              Mermaidens, naked
   at the nipples and below, still
   mate with sailors in their sleep.

And who escapes from sleep?
Waken, and you wage one ship
  against the aces of the sea.
Weaken, and the bait of Faust's bad
  wager waits you.
                    Worsen,
  and the winds of old indulgence
overtake you.
                    You face them
  as you'd face, years afterward,
  a girl you kissed and fondled
  in a park but never married.
Becalmed, you make your peace
  with dreams.
                    Expect nothing,
  and anything seems everything.
Expect everything, and anything
  seems nothing.
                    To live
  you leave your yesterselves
  to drown without a funeral.
You chart a trek where no
  one's sailed before.
                    You rig.
You anchor up.
                    You sail.

For Karl, the Cornell rower,
  who wore the medals he deserved.
For Grogan of Brooklyn, who left
  no memory worth mentioning.
For Foley, who married the Commandant's
  daughter though nothing came of it.
For Clasby, who wanted out,
  and when he could, got out.
For Schoen, who married, stayed in,
  thickened, and retired a colonel.
For Chalfant, who bought a sword
  and dress blues but remained Chalfant.
For Billy Adrian, the best
  of punters, haunted by Korea.
For Nick Christopolos, who kept
  a luger, just in case.
For Soderberg, who taught us
  songs on the hot Sundays.
For Dahlstrom, the tennis king,
  who starched his dungarees erect.
For Jacobson, who followed me
  across the worst of all creeks.
For Laffin and the gun he cracked
  against a rock and left there.
For Nathan Hale, who really was
  descended but shrugged it off.
For Elmore, buried in Yonkers
  five presidents ago.
For Lonnie MacMillan, who spoke
  his Alabamian mind regardless.
For Bremser of Yale, who had it
  and would always have it.
For lean Clyde Lee, who stole
  from Uncle once too often.

For Dewey Ehling and the clarinet
  he kept but never played.
For Lockett of the Sugar Bowl
  champs, and long may he run.
For Lyle Beeler, may he rot
  as an aide to the aide of an aide.
For Joe Buergler, who never
  would pitch in the majors.
For Kerg, who called all women cows
  but married one who wasn't.
For me, who flunked each
  test on weapons but the last.
For Sheridan, who flunked them all,
  then goofed the battle games
  by leaving his position, hiding
  in a pine above the generals'
  latrine until he potted
  every general in sight, thus
  stopping single-handedly the war.

DON JUAN'S DREAM OF NEAR
AND FAR MISSES

Your wenching done, you dreamed
  alive your score of paramours:
  she with the whore's lips, she
  from the shore, she with the tanned
  hips, she with real panthers
  staring from her eyes, she
  of the whips and mirrors....

                      All
  these you numbered to your skills
  like scalps or notches on a rifle
  stock or stenciled emblems
  of the sun across a fuselage.
Was every girl herself
  or who you dreamed she was?
In Montreal she whispered "No,
  no, no, no, no."

              In Alexandria
  she plucked her eyebrows in the nude.
In Rome she never gave
  her name.

          Each time you found
  and took her, she became herself
  anew in someone else.

               Was she
  Yvonne, who never kissed by day,
  or Evelyn, who tangoed you to death?
And what of the twins from Spain?
You offered Ava Eva's ring
  engraved with Eva's name
  on Ava's anniversary.

When trouble
doubled, you resolved to choose
the mate who'd save you from yourself.
Docile you would have her, schooled
in deference, religious to a point
but not averse to dalliance.
She of the king's inheritance?
Already spoken for.
                    She
without attachments?
                          Dying
in Lugano.
              She who had called
you casual?
                    Your letter came back
burned....
                    At last the Home for Old
Lotharios admitted you.
                          Nuns
assisted you with slippers, pills
and liniments.
                    You saw fresh
universes in their faces, not two
the same but all beyond you.
By night you learned again
that loins were loins.
                          Blinder
than revenge, they made their own
decisions.
                    You showered in ice water,
practiced Zen, saltpetered
all your meals.

Hair-shirted
in your cell, you vowed before
the god of all lost loves
that you would never take
that road again, that you
would take that road never
again, that you would take never
that road again.
                    Halfway down
the road, you kept repeating that.

NAPOLEON'S

Appropriate that near the tomb
　of Bonaparte, upended cannon
　barrels should defend the corridors.
This Corsican who loved artillery
　would surely have condoned such vigilance.
"Give them a whiff of grape,"
　he muttered once before he fired
　at a mob with scattershot.
　　　　　　　　　　　To crack
　an enemy's defense he nixed
　direct assaults as rapes.
　　　　　　　　　Instead,
　he concentrated all his cannon power
　on the weakest of the weakest flanks
　of that defense until it cracked.
Accepting losses with a lover's
　shrug, he claimed that Paris
　could replace them in a single night.
At Waterloo, the rain, not Wellington,
　defeated him.
　　　　　　　　Unable to maneuver
　caissons in the mud, he damned
　the French, the English and himself
　to history.
　　　　　　　That history engraves
　the upright cannon shaft that he
　erected in the Place Vendome
　from all the melted guns of Austerlitz.
Centering the square, it scrolls
　in corkscrew chapters to its tip
　a bronze procession of the passionate
　in arms....

Outside the Ritz,
a newsgirl pedals by, her nipples
tenting a *Herald-Tribune*
T-shirt sweated to her breasts.
Tour guides and all guided near
the pillar glance away from France
to study what is after all
quite clearly in a manner of speaking
also a piece of the tale of France.
Aroused and rising to a war
they think they'll win, a few
stragglers, squinting at their target's
front and flanks, change
suddenly to cannoneers and zero in.

WAITING FOR ZERO

Confirming that the avant-garde
   can't wait for history, gray Hemingway
reached Paris seven days before
the Liberation.
                    With Nazis near
the Place Vendome, he freed
his moveable feast and waited
for the troops....
                    Like Hemingway you wait
for snow before a January second
masquerading as the first of May.
The maple buds almost believe it.
Stallion dung around a pear tree
   thaws into its pasture smell
again.
         Even a buried crocus
lets its periscope break ground.
So far, no snow.
               Whether
it will come or go is in
the winds of Canada.
                    But you....
You act as if it's here.
                    Your blood's
already down to three below.
Your shoulders chill and heighten
in the winds to come.
                    Remembering
your future as a fact, you turtle up
like any seed beneath the snow
or like a snoozing black bear
in the hills and wait for Easter,
wait for history....

But just suppose
the wait's too long and troublesome.
Or else suppose that Easter's
not enough—or not at all.
Which brings you back to Hemingway
in Idaho in 1961.
                    His feast
no longer moveable, his hunter's
eyes too sick to see, his future
certain to grow worse, he faced
the choice of waiting for the end
or not.
            At last he thought
ahead of how it felt to be
the first to Paris.
                    Then,
he held the muzzle cold
between his teeth and bit and shot.

A CITY MADE SACRED BECAUSE YOUR SON'S GRANDFATHER DIED IN IT

Your father in a wheelchair slouches
   steeply to his stroked-out side.
Your son wheels for the final
   time his final grandfather.
And you, who've walked this street
   so many times you know
   the slope and crack of every
   sidewalk square, just walk
   behind.
            You ask your son
   (or is it just your son?)
   to slow things down.
                  Your father flicks his good
   right hand to say he can't
   accept but won't deny what's
   happened, that not accepting
   what is unacceptable is all
   life meant or means to him.
You want to hold his other
   hand and squeeze it back
   to life until the doctors
   and their facts relent.
                  The doctors
   and their facts go on.
                  So do
   the unaffected riders in the numbered
   buses.
            So does the whole
   damn city that becomes no more
   than just a place to live
   and die in now.

The more you walk,
the less you know the street
you knew.
            The less you know,
the more the curbs become
opposing shores.
            The street
is suddenly the river no man
steps in twice or finally outswims.
Midway between your father
and your son, you feel yourself
drawn in and on and under.

THE BEARING

Heavy from her steady bellying,
  the mare comes due.
                    No memory
of ten Kentuckies or the horse farms
east of Buffalo prepares you
for the silk of that first fur.
You've seen the Easter foals stilting
  in toy gallops by their almost
inattentive mothers.
                  You've known
from watching what the breeding
of Arabia will hone from all
that spindliness: in weeks the fetlocks
shapelier; in months the girth below
the withers sinewed like a harp;
in years the stance and prancing
that will stop a crowd.
                 But now the colt's nose nudging
for horse milk nullifies a dream
to come of stallions.
            Now
it is enough to know that something
can arrive so perfectly and stand
upright among so many fallen
miracles and, standing, fill
the suddenly all-sacred barn
with trumpets and a memory of kings.

Denying what it means to doubt,
   this year's forsythias unfold
   and flood the air with yellow
   answers.
            They say it's time
   I opened up, time I learned
   French, time I liked less
   and loved more, time
   I listened to the sun, time
   I made time.
               Why not?
Can days of making sense
   of days that make no sense
   make sense?
               If nothing's sure
   but nothing's sure, then reading
   Montesquieu must wait.
Preparing for my enemies must
   wait.
         And gravity the hurrier
   must wait because forsythias
   are happening.
               They make me
   turn my back on forts,
   insurance policies, inoculations,
   wire barbed or braided,
   bodyguards and all the folderol
   of fear.
            They say that this
   year's blossoms will outlive
   the lasting death of Mars.
There are no flowers on the stars.

For Grace (7/19/78)

LEAFING

Bagged and burned, they turn
  into the only smoke that's worth
  the tasting.
              Woods revert
  to wood as I, their janitor,
  rake up the year.
              Cleansed,
  cleansed to my tree of bones
  and savoring the blown tobacco
  of November, I recall Chateaubriand's
  "Forests precede civilizations,
  but deserts follow them."
Disturbing comments for a ballpoint
  era where psychiatry's the state
  religion, and the prize of prizes
  is a champagne shampoo
  in the locker room.
              My woods
  are far from forests, but I know
  real deserts when I see them.
So I work my bonewood rake,
  leafing for reasons to repudiate
  Chateaubriand.
              The answer's
  in the trees.
              Shorn to their shells,
  they'll wait the winter out
  and start all over when
  the time is right.
              By then
  the desert's prize and predecessors
  will have gone the way of smoke.
As long as there's a leaf, there's hope.

Wing to wing, they bake
  in weather than can sizzle bacon
  on their stars.
                    Fighters, bombers,
  trainers—Arizona stores them all
  unrusting in a prophecy of yesterday.
West by half the Pacific, the holy
  salvage of another Arizona
  consecrates Pearl Harbor like a church.
If wreckages were pages, nothing
  could book them.
                    Cain's garbage
  mines the Baltic, fouls
  forty years of bracken near
  Cassino, spoils Guam's lagoon.
What were these havocs to their crews
  but new toys for an old game?
As facts left over from a fact,
  they speak for history ahead
  of all that history remembers
  to predict about the tactics of our kind.
Cain's rock and rocket
  leave us nothing new to find.
In North America the oldest skull's
  a woman's, brained from behind.

THE NEXT TIME YOU WERE THERE

After Paris, every city's just
  another town.
                   Elephants could roam
  the Metro, Marly's horses
  could invade the Tuileries, wishbone
  arches on the Seine could shatter
  under traffic, and Parisians could
  refuse to estivate in August....
Appearing every day in Paris
  would be Haussmann's Paris still.
Abroad, you'd like to die the way
  you live in Paris—telescoping four
  days into three, believing that your best
  is just ahead, protesting
  that you need more time, more time,
  protesting to the end.
                   And past
  the end....
              But you exaggerate.
This capital you share with France
  is just another web—somewhere
  to breathe and board and be.
You bring there what you are,
  and what you are is nowhere
  any different.
            This makes
  the Trocadero just a penny's patch
  of grass, the Place de la Concorde
  a wide and spindled planisphere,
  and St. Germaine-des-Prés another
  church.

Weathering your dreams,
bronze Paris of the doorknobs
turns into the turning stage
called here that stays the same
as everywhere right now.
On that
quick stage a man keeps happening.
From Paris to Paris to Paris,
the only life he knows
is anywhere and always coming
true....
His name is you.

"Black dog" was Churchill's
  phrase for what I'm facing
  here.
          I keep reporting
  to my desk, my pen, my books,
  but nothing comes of it.
I'm spared confirming Montesquieu's
  "A man can play the fool
  in everything but poetry."
I'm out of poetry right now.
Seamus would shrug and say,
  "When you have nothing to write,
  write nothing."
                  Better than
  writing badly.
                  Better than fraud.
On T-shirts, matchbooks and bumper
  stickers, fraud has risen
  to final solutions.
                  "Send
  a Cuban home for Christmas!"
"Sickle-cell anemia's
  the great white hope!"
"Arabs can go and reproduce
  themselves."
          The isms
  in the words explode like spittle
  in my face....
                  If all we do
  begins in our imagining, I should
  expect the worst more often than
  the best.

It sells.

It meets the needs

of hate.

It happens on command.

It lacks the lightning of the best,
which comes when it comes to write
the man the way a dance
will dance the dancers when the dance
is right.

Like love it lets
the eyes become the face's
sky again and takes us where
it takes us—never soon
enough but not too late.
As long as that's worth
waiting for, I'll wait.

It's been expecting me so long
　that I feel late.
　　　　　　　Dropped
stones are what it's thirsty for,
and I've come armed....
　　　　　　　　　I hear
the ghosts of splashes plummet
upward like the tired swallows
of a heart near death.
　　　　　　　If I
could dunk and hoist a bucket,
I would taste what mountain
brooks remember of the snow.
Instead, I whisper down
　my name, my name, my name
　and listen as it yoyos
　in a rounding echo back,
　back, back....
　　　　　　Below the parapet
　the swirling walls dive
　farther down than I can dream.
Deeper, where night and water
　meet, the moon of the assassins
　waits for yesterday and never sleeps.

I say what Lindbergh's father
  said to Lindbergh: "One boy's
  a boy; two boys are half
  a boy; three boys are no
  boy at all."
            Which helps explain
why Lindbergh kept his boyishness
for life, which meant he stayed
himself, which means a lot.
What else is destiny?
            After
  you learn that governments lie
  and happiness is undefinable
  and death has no patience,
  you'll understand me.
            Meanwhile
  the ignorant but well-informed
  will try to keep you mute
  as a shut book.
          Forecasters of the best
and worst will hurry to retreat
infallibly into the future.
           Ministers
who talk on cue with God
will weigh you down like serious
furniture.
        Assume that what
you lose to such distractions
you will gain in strength.
By then you'll learn that all
  you know will help you less
  than how you think.

The rest
is memory, and memory's the graveyard
of the mind as surely as tomorrow
is its myth.
            Nowhere but the time
at hand is when you'll see
that God's geometry is feast
enough.
            Within the world's
closed circles, everything's
the sum of halves that rhyme.
From coconuts to butterflies
to lovers knotted on the soft
battlefield of any bed, the halves
add up to one, and every
one remembers where it came
from as a trumpet note
recalls the song it was a part of
and the listeners who heard it
and were changed.
            What Lindbergh's
father meant and what I mean
are two roads to the same
country.
            Knowing how long
it takes us to be young, he left
his son some clues to get
his bearings by.
            And so do I.

What absence only can create
  needs absence to create it.
Split by deaths or distances,
  we all survive like exiles
    from the time at hand, living
    where love leads us for love's
    reasons.
          We tell ourselves
that life, if anywhere, is there.
Why isn't it?
           What keeps us
  hostages to elsewhere?
               The dead
  possess us when they choose.
The far stay nearer than we know
  they are.
          We taste the way
they talk, remember everything
they've yet to tell us, dream
them home and young again
from countries they will never leave.
With friends it's worse and better.
Together, we regret the times
  we were apart.
            Apart, we're
more together than we are
together.
          We say that losing
those we love to living
is the price of loving.

We say
such honest lies because
we must—because we have
no choices.
                    Face to face
we say them, but our eyes
have different voices.

I'm tired of living for tomorrow's
   headlines, tired of explanations,
   tired of letters that begin "Dear
   patriot..." or else "You may
   already be the winner of...."
I'm near the point where nothing's
   worth the time.
                        The causes
   I believe in rarely win.
The men and women I admire
   most are quietly ignored.
What's called "the infinite
   progression of the negative" assumes
   if I can count to minus seven,
   I can count to minus seven
   million, which means the bad
   can certainly get worse, and that
   the worse can certainly, et cetera....
Regardless, I believe
   that something in me always was
   and will be what I am.
I make each day my revolution.
Each revolution is a wheel's full
   turn where nothing seems the same
   while everything's no different.
I want to shout in every dialect
   of silence that the world we dream
   is what the world becomes,
   and what the world's become
   is there for anyone's re-dreaming.
Even the vanishing of facts
   demands a consecration: the uncolor
   of champagne, the way that presidential

signatures remind me of a heartbeat's
dying scrawl across a monitor,
the languages that earlobes speak
when centered by enunciating pearls,
the sculpture of a limply belted
dress, the instant of bite
when grapes taste grape.
                                        The range
of plus is no less infinite
than minus....
                              I learn that going
on means coming back
and looking hard at just one thing.
That rosebush, for example.
A single rose on that bush.
The whiteness of that rose.
                                        A petal
of that whiteness.
                              The tip
of that petal.
                        The curl of that tip.
And just like that the rose
in all its whiteness blooms
within me like a dream so true
that I can taste it.
                        And I do.

"When your son has grown up,
treat him like your brother."
Arab proverb

Don't wait for definitions.
                        I've had
    my fill of aftertalk
    and overtalk, of meanings that don't
    mean, of words not true
    enough to be invisible, of all
    those Januaries of the mind when
    everything that happens happens
    from the eyebrows up.
                        If truth
    is in the taste and not
    the telling, give me whatever
    is and cannot be again—
    like sherbet on the tongue, like love....
Paris defined is Paris
    lost, but Paris loved
    is always Orly in the rain,
    broiled pork and chestnuts
    near the Rue de Seine,
    the motorcade that sped de Gaulle
    himself through Montparnasse.
                        Viva
    the fool who said, "Show me
    a man who thinks, I'll show
    you a man who frowns."
                        Which
    reminds me of Andrew learning
    to count by twos and asking,
    "Where is the end of counting?"

Let's settle for the salt and pepper
    of the facts.
                    Oranges don't parse,
and no philosopher can translate
shoulders in defeat or how
it feels when luck's slim arrow
stops at you or why lovemaking's
not itself until it's made.
Let's breathe like fishermen who sit
    alone together on a dock
    and let the wind do all
    the talking.
                    That way we'll see
that who we are is what
we'll be hereafter.
                    We'll learn
the bravery of trees that cannot
know "the dice of God
are always loaded."
                    We'll think
of life as one long kiss
since talk and kisses never mix.
We'll watch the architecture
    of the clouds create themselves
    like flames and disappear like laughter.

The Arabs of Andalús bequeathed
  the troubadours a minstrelsy
  where love and passion sang.
Latins ignored the song.
Gaius Valerius Catullus
  and his tribe preferred coupling
  on impulse and praising it in couplets
afterward.
                    The mix created
courtly love.
                    From courtly love
came all the legends of romance,
and from romance the dream where love
of passion seemed more impassioned
than the passion of love.
                              Still, we must
be fair.
            Though wiving and wenching
gave way to wiving or wenching,
a few still lived the passionate
friendship that is marriage.
                              But
most remained as permanently
parallel as railroad tracks
that never meet except
at the horizon.
                    And even there
it's an illusion.
                    No wonder
choosing one another every
day became a chore while coupling
on the sly assumed the guise
of ecstasy.

But why be righteous?
We've lovers all, and love
  without responsibility is every lover's
  dream of happiness.
                        Yet all
  that lasts is not what prompts
  but what survives the act.
                        If man's
  a wallet waiting to be spent,
  the question's never whether
  but with whom.
                  And why.
                        If woman
  is a purse whose body's mouths
  are drawstrung shut until
  she gives herself away,
  the question's never whether
  but with whom.
                  And why.
                        The Arabs
  thought the why unsayable and sang
  the beauties of the where and when.
Catullus settled for the how.
Both felt they sang the answer then
  for something unexplainable
  before.
              Or since.
                  Or now.

The fifty-year-old girl of twenty
   said, "In love it's best
   to be cynical."
               She'd modeled, acted
   in French commercials and sung
   rock with a group called
   "Soviet Sex."
               Her eyes were cat's
   eyes but without the mystery.
Her smile faded like tired foam
   or like a memory of Berryman,
   who, when all he spoke and wrote
   was poetry, decided he was through.
That's how it ends with some.
Burn fast, burn out....
                  Even
   the repenters live clichés
   that guarantee oblivion.
                  Grundy,
   who put himself through college
   selling marijuana, prosecutes
   for Justice now in Washington.
Eldridge Cleaver shouts
   like Billy Sunday.
               Nixon's
   cronies milk the lecture
   circuit, publish fiction
   and believe with all their re-born
   might in President Jesus....
I think like this while watching
   lightning bugs play midnight
   tag around my house.

                    Ignite
and pause.
                    Ignite and pause—
each one its own Prometheus,
a sun in flight, a type
of Edison.
                    They burn like signals
hyphenated by the breath of night.
Each time I think they're burning out
    instead of on, they burn again
    like pulses that will just not die.
Their brightness lightens me.
It's no small thing to bear
    a dawn within you.
                    It's
even more at midnight to create
with nothing but your being
plus a light that tunes the darkness
something like the music of the sky.

October's ochre changes
  everything to Italy.
                          Sunpainted
walls remember villas
from Fiesole.
                 I've never seen
Fiesole.
          Some day I will,
and it will seem a memory
of noon in the United States
when I became a Florentine
because the sun bewildered me.
Who among the Florentines
  is listening?
               Who else but me
who sees in the Italians
"the human race" that Goethe
  saw....
           Today their cops
are commodores; their Fiats,
weapons in their whizzing duels
on the road; their shoes and gloves,
the very renaissance of calf.
Tribal to the death, they swear
  by their mothers, breast-feed
  their sons wherever, prefer
  their pasta three-fourths cooked,
  and sing whatever whenever....
Mistaken for Italian half
  my life, I'm of the tribe.
If it's Italian to speak
  in tears before goodbyes,
  I qualify.

If it's Italian
to choose tomatoes one
by one, I qualify.
                    If it's
Italian to laugh when no one
else is laughing or to whistle
at the wheel, I qualify.
                    One
murmur in Italian soothes
the Florentine in me that French
confuses, German contradicts,
and Spanish misses by a hair.
One murmur, and I feel
what Goethe felt when Florence
wounded him with Italy
for life though Goethe spent
not quite three hours there.

KAK

Her heroines were Pola Negri,
  Gloria Swanson and Mae West—
  one for glamour, one for style,
  one for nerve.
              First on her scale
  of praise came courage of the heart,
  then brains, then something called
  in Arabic "lightbloodedness."
                          All
  birds but owls she loved, all
  that was green and growable,
  including weeds, all operas
  in Italian, the schmaltzier the better....
Lightning she feared, then age
  since people thought the old
  "unnecessary," then living on
  without us, then absolutely nothing.
Each time I'd say some girl
  had perfect legs, she'd tell me
  with a smile, "Marry her legs."
Of if I'd find a project
  difficult, she'd say, "Your mother,
  Lottie, mastered Greek
  in seven months."
                  Or once
  when Maris bested Ruth's
  home runs by one, she said,
  "Compared to Ruth, who's Harris?"
Crying while she stitched my shirt,
  she said, "You don't know
  what to suffer is until
  someone you love is suffering
  to death, and what can you do?"

On principle she told one bishop
   what she thought of him.
On personality she called one
   global thinker temporarily
   insane.
            She dealt a serious
   hand of poker, voted
   her last vote for Kennedy,
   and wished us a son two years
   before he came.
            She hoped
   that she would never die
   in bed.
            And never she did.
"When you and your brother were young,"
   she said, "and I was working,
   then was I happy."
            And she was.
The folderol of funerals disgusted
   her enough to say, "I'm
   telling no one when
   I die."
            And she didn't.
One night she jotted down
   in longhand on a filing card,
   "I pray to God that I'll be
   with you always."
            And she is.

We speak as people in motion
  speak, more sure of what's
  behind us than ahead,
  but going anyway.
                    Trying to see
  beyond the world we see,
  we see that seeing's dangerous.
Our props collapse.
                    Religion,
  custom, law, the dream
  called government....
                    Nothing
  sustains us but our eyes and what
  our eyes, by saying nothing,
  say.
        No wonder Timmerman
  could claim for all of us,
  "I'm more at home in subjects
  now, not countries."
                    Before
  the real frontiers, our passports
  are invalid.
                    They tell us
  how we're called but never
  who we are, and who we are's
  the mystery.
                    The pilgrim in us
  has no fixed address.
                    He roams.
He takes us with him when
  he goes.

Encowled within
a fuselage, we speed toward
a short tomorrow in another
world.
       We land, speak languages
we almost understand and trust
in strangers as the best of friends,
and for a time they are.
                Years
afterward we feel a bond
with them so indestructible
that we're amazed.
           If they
should die, we'd grieve for them
like those old Cuban fishermen
who grieved for Hemingway because
he fished the gulf they fished
and called them friends.
             With nothing
else to offer him, they gave
the bronze propellers of their
very boats for melting to create
his statue in the plaza of Cojimar….
For us the best memorials
are what we heard or read
en route.
      "He's old, but still
in life."
      "Nothing but heart
attack kill Christophine, but why
in that box she so swell up?"
"Cruelty's a mystery and a waste
of pain."

"I like a dog
that makes you think when you
look at him."
        "*El Cordobés es
un hombre muy valiente.*"
                        Each word's
a time.
            Each time's a place.
Each place is where a time
  repeats itself because a word
  returns us there.
                    Crisscrossing
through the universe the way
that lightning diagrams the sky,
we're all companions of the road
at different altitudes.
                    Here
in my speeding house below
the speeding stars, I'm turning
into language from a pen while you're
confiding in some traveler you'll
never see again.
                The quiet
bronze of words remembers us.
                        It says
we were, we are, we will be.

If "life's a dream with doubts
    about itself," the dreaming
    never stops.
                    Regretting
what you did or did not do
    or always wished to do adds up
    to who you are....
                        Piaf pretended
she regretted nothing.
                    One
genius in his epitaph regretted
    only he was not "the man
    in whose embrace Mathilde Urbach
    swooned."
                    One emperor with no
regrets in middle age
    regretted having no regrets.
Translated, these examples say
    no life is long enough
    nor cosmopolitan enough nor anything
    enough.
                    If you desire to see
your son's daughter's son's
    daughter, you want no less
    than anybody wants.
                        Or if you thirst
to visit everywhere in every
    hemisphere, you mimic old Batuta's
    passion for the next horizon.
Or if you hunger for the maximum,
    you're Faust with all of Faust's
    excesses to remember....

                    So much
for dreams.
                If you want something
to regret, why not regret you never
once opposed some fluent undermen
we manage to elect—the ideology
or sociology or therapy that people
eat as poetry—the arguments
about theology whose final argument
is *who's the boss*—the righteous
tribes for whom the Renaissance might
just as well have never happened?
Why did you never say that one
good student's worth a thousand
senators?
                Or that one carpenter
outskills the slitherings of advertisers,
diplomats, and other oilers of the word?
Between what you remember
or presume, you're in translation
by whatever keeps translating April
into May, decisions into consequences,
fathers into sons, and you
into whatever.
                I know
the circumstance.
                    I'm you,
and both of us keep planning
for tomorrow while we're turning
into yesterday.
                What else
can we conclude except we grow
and die in place despite
our dreams?

          What is our bounty
but the permanent impermanence
of breath, a shared invisibility,
a gift?
          What is our peace
but stopping as we go and talking
for a while of that, just
that, translation to translation?

It's time you paganized yourself
  and left all sublimations
  to the dry of soul.
               It's time
  you learned that ears can taste,
  and eyes remember and the tongue
  and nostrils see like fingertips
  in any dark.
            Think back
  or look around, and all you know
  is what your body taught you:
  lake smoke in the Adirondacks,
  the razor's flame across
  your lathered cheek, language
  that changed to silence or to tears
  when there was nothing more
  to say....
          Right here in Cannes
  on the Fourth of July, you watch
  a cornucopia a-swelter in the sun.
A Saudi wife, enrobed
  and cowled like a nun, passes
  a Cannaise in her isosceles
  and thong.
          They stand there
  like opposed philosophies of women,
  history, desire, God
  and everything you think about
  too much....
         The stationed candles
  on the altar of Notre Dame
  de Bon Voyage diminish
  like your future.

Anchored
in the bay, the *S.S. Ticonderoga*
claims the future's now.
Housing a zillion dollars'
  worth of hardware in her hull,
  she's programmed for the war
  that no one wants.
                    She bristles
  like a ploughshare honed into a sword—
  the ultra-weapon from the ultra-tool.
Basking in the hull of your skin
  that shields the software of yourself
  against the worst, you contemplate
  the carefully united states
  you call your body.
                    Concealed
  or bared, it houses who you are,
  and who you are is why you live,
  and why you live is worth
  the life it takes to wonder how.
Your body's not concerned.
                          It answers
  what it needs with breath, sleep,
  love, sweat, roses,
  children and a minimum of thought.
It says all wars are waged
  by puritans, and that the war
  nobody wants is history's excuse
  or every war that ever happened....
The gray Ticonderoga fires
  a salute of twenty guns
  plus one for independence
  and the men who died to earn it.

Each shot reminds you of the killed
    Americans still left in France.
Before they left their bodies,
    did they think of war or what
    their bodies loved and missed
    the most: a swim at noon,
    the night they kissed a woman
    on her mouth, the dawns they waited
    for the wind to rise like music,
    or the simple freedom of a walk,
    a waltz, a trip?
                    Under
    the sun of Cannes, you hum
    your mind to sleep.
                    You tell
    yourself that time is one
    day long or one long day
    with pauses for the moon and stars,
    and that tomorrow's sun is yesterday's
    today.
            Your body answers
    that it knows, it's known
    for years, it's always known.

Each dawn I slew the sand
  behind Grand Case toward
  the cape where Jackie O
  is building her alternative.
                        Upbeach,
  two naked mermaids snorkel
  through the surf, their backs
  awash with ocean suds, their gleaming
  bottoms, like O'Murphy's, dolphining
  in tandem as their finned feet
  churn.
              A poem I've been planning
  pulls apart.
                  The more I mine
  for nouns and fish for verbs
  the more it pulls apart.
                        By noon
  the almost breathing sea assumes
  the fully female languor
  of a woman sleeping naked
  on the beach—her breasts adjusting
  as she turns, her thighs dividing
  like abandonment itself, her mating
  slot so free of shame it shows
  its secret to the sun.
                        I tell
  myself I'm here like Jackie O,
  and for a week it's true.
                        The time
  is always sun o'clock, and every
  day is Sunday.

The nights
are stars and coffee and a netted
bed.
      But all around me live
black men with Dutch and French
and Spanish names and blood
so mixed that all the scars
of slavery bleed through.
                    Daily
they show me history in sepia.
That history's defunct and all
the slavers sunk, but still
the only church is Catholic Dutch.
The menus mimic Europe,
and a drunk whose middle name
is Van distributes all the Heinekens
in town.
            But who am I
to criticize?
                An ex-colonial myself,
I can't distinguish custom
in my life from conscience, and I
end half-Calvinist, half-hedonist
with nothing to confess but
contradiction.
                  Island or mainland,
what's the difference?
                      Until
a poem I cannot deny denudes
me into life, I'm just another
pilgrim passing through the obvious.
I need a true alternative
where now is never long

enough to write down what
I know.
        Instead I stay a tan
away from who I was a hemisphere
ago.
        I'm western history
revisited.
        I'm souvenirs and sun
revisited.
        I pay my way and go.

Killarney's maps are for the unredeemed.
The hidden land awaits the stumblers
  and the temporarily confused who find
  their destinations as they go.
In Dingle there's a history
  bone-final as the faith
  that founded Gallarus.
                All
  that remains is what was there
  when Gallarus began: God,
  man, sheep and stone
  and stone and stone.
              Dingles
  ago the starvers saw their lips
  turn green from chewing grass
  before they famished in their beds.
Their hovels bleach like tombs
  unroofed and riven by the sea.
If only all the stones were beige
  or marble-white....
              Their fading
  grays seem unforgiving as a fate
  that only wit or tears
  or emigration can defeat.
Sheep graze over graves.
Loud gulls convene on garbage
  dumps.
          In Galway, Cashel
  and Tralee, I fish the air
  for what it is that makes
  the Irish Irish.
             Is it Seamus
  speaking Sweeney's prayer

in Howth and telling me of Hopkins,
"the convert," buried in Glasnevin?
Is it how it sounds to sing
   the music in a name: Skibbereen,
   Balbriggan, Kilbeggan, Bunratty,
   Listowel, Duncannon, Fermanagh
   and Ballyconneely?
                              Is it Joyce's
   map of metaphors that makes
   all Dublin mythical as Greece?
Is it cairns of uniambic and unrhyming
   rocks transformed by hand
   into the perfect poem of a wall?
Is it the priest near death
   who whispered, "Give my love
   to Roscommon, and the horses
   of Roscommon?"
                           Is it because
   the Irish pray alike for "Pope
   John Paul, our bishop Eamon, and
   Ned O'Toole, late of Moycullen?"
Inside God's house or out
   their sadder smiles say the world,
   if given time, will break your heart.
With such a creed they should
   believe in nothing but the wisdom
   of suspicion.
                        Instead they say,
   "Please God," and fare ahead
   regardless of the odds to show
   that life and God deserve at least
   some trust, some fearlessness, some courtesy.

For Anne Mullin Burnham

People you will never want to know
   are telling you to vote, enlist,
   invest, travel to Acapulco,
   buy now and pay later, smoke,
   stop smoking, curb your dog,
   remember the whale and praise
   the Lord.
                  Like windshield wipers
   they repeat themselves.
                               Because
   they tell but never ask, you learn
   to live around them just to live.
You understand why Paul Gauguin
   preferred Tahiti to the bourgeoisie
   of France.
                  But then Tahiti's
   not the answer anymore,
   and frankly never was.
                           This leaves
   you weighing Schulberg's waterfront
   philosophy: "You do it to him
   before he does it to you."
Reactionary, you admit, but nature's
   way, the way of this world
   where he who wins is always
   he who loses least and last....
But if you're bored by triumph
   through attrition, imitate you may
   the strategy of Puck.
                           Listen
   carefully to all solicitations, smile
   and respond in classical Greek.

It's devious, but then it gives
　　you time to smell the always
　　breathing flowers.
　　　　　　　　Or to watch
　　dissolve into the mystery of coffee
　　the faceless dice of sugar
　　cubes.
　　　　　　Or to say how damn
　　remarkable it is that every
　　evening somewhere in this world
　　a play of Shakespeare's being staged
　　with nothing to be won but excellence.

TO ALL MY MARINERS IN ONE

Forget the many who talk
   much, say little, mean
   less and matter least.
                              Forget
   we live in times when broadcasts
   of Tchaikovsky's Fifth precede
   announcements of the death
   of tyrants.
                         Forget that life
   for governments is priced
   war-cheap but kidnap-high.
Our seamanship is not with such.
From port to port we learn
   that "depths last longer
   than heights," that years are
   meant to disappear like wakes,
   that nothing but the sun stands
   still.
               We share the sweeter
   alphabets of laughter and the slower
   languages of pain.
                              Common
   as coal, we find in one another's
   eyes the quiet diamonds
   that are worth the world.
                                 Drawn
   by the song of our keel, what
   are we but horizons coming true?
Let others wear their memories
   like jewelry.
                       We're of the few
   who work apart so well,
   together when we must.

                          We speak
    cathedrals when we speak
    and trust no promise but
    the pure supremacy of tears.
                              What
    more can we expect?
                          The sea's
    blue mischief may be waiting
    for its time and place, but still
    we have the stars to guide us.
    We have the wind for company.
    We have ourselves.
                      We have
    a sailor's faith that says
    not even dying can divide us.

AFTER MERCUTIO

Come we to this commemoration
nude or garbed, we stay
in most ways one.
Midnight
enshrouds us, and the moon enrobes us
gray and silver to the galaxies.
Black lawns await the sun
to paint them green again.
The sick are for a time sleep-spared
the cruelty of roses.
Swimming
a sweeter dark, a lover
lets his fingertips be eyes
until the lolling one he teases
sheaths and thighs him to herself.
The kiss of bellies is their
everything.
Elsewhere in the easy
cladding of her skin, a showered
wife looks west.
Whatever
she's observing is composing her.
Cats are afoot.
Their arch
stares sparkle sapphire
in the shadows.
Listen.
Volcanoes
in the sea are spewing ash.
We overhear them as the deaf
hear detonations with their eyes.
Chocked attics whisper
to themselves like thieves in corridors.

Isled in the sunlight of the seafall
  moon, we beachcomb where we choose
  while everything around us
  turns into itself.
                Because
a willow wavers, we believe
in wind, believe in stars
ensorcelled by the same wind,
believe ourselves believing.
We praise the perfect poem
  of a hen's each egg.
                Platters
of wet grapes in loose
erotic sprawls seem irresistible
as kisses.
           Rivers arouse
and reach within us oceans
far beyond our fathoming.
When we're made mad enough
  by all this sorcery, we dance
  fandangos on the shore before
  we sleep.
           Or else we sing
the hymn that David sang to Saul
until the old king woke
and walked.
           The world deserves
that little….
          Nightwords
like these are not for those
who love the lies of triumph
that prevail as history.

                    They're
for the fools who pry from mystery
some memory of who we are
and why we're here.
                    They're for
the mildly bemused and wildly
free.
        For you.
                    For me.

Downstairs a trumpeter is playing
  Gershwin badly but somehow
  truer that way.
              The squat
chimney of my pipe keeps offering
smoke signals to the moon.
The sea-waves glitter like a zillion
  nickels....
              Two wars ago
  the battle of the Riviera happened
  here.
      Two wars ago
  the author of *The Little Prince*
  flew southward from this coast
  and crashed at sea without a trace.
That's how I tell the time
  these days—by wars, the madness
  of wars.
              I think of Mussolini,
  who believed each generation
  needed war to purify its blood.
He leaned on history to show
  that life's unlivable except
  through death.
              I palm the ashes
from my pipe.
              To hell
with Mussolini.
              I'll take
bad Gershwin to a bullet
any time.

To hell with history.
The moon's manna on the sea
  outshines the glory that was Greece.
To hell with those who say
  the earth's a battleground we're doomed
  to govern with a gun.
                                Because
  of them we have to fight to live.
But win or lose, they've won
  since fighting proves they're right.
Why ask if they outnumber us
  or not?
            It just takes one.

MATADOR

"He killed dying, and he died killing."
*Translation of the headline announcing the
death of Manolete, August 28, 1948*

"Are my eyes open, Doctor? I can't see."
Last words of Manolete

The photographs survive.
                    He stands
  at sentinel's attention in his suit
  of lights.
                His cape encowls him
  like a crimson wing.
                        Kneeling
  before the snout or kissing
  the horn of a bled and broken
  bull he thought undignified.
                            Instead
  he faced the black fury
  of the beast at full strength,
  steering him from miss to miss
  until the sacrifice.
                    His art
  was not to fight but to conduct
  the bull the way a maestro
  might conduct an orchestra.
                        With death
  as close as God or love,
  he worked his cape like a baton
  and never moved his feet....
He never moved his feet.
No wonder they revere his melancholy
    courage to this very day
      in Córdoba, Madrid and Mexico.
And they have reason.

Even
the ones who hate the spectacle
respect the man who braved so
much without a backward step.
Forget the fame, the mistress
and the fortune in pesetas.

Can these
explain why someone heeds
a calling that allows as many
victories as possible but only
one defeat?

What each of us
evades until the end, he faced
twelve hundred times alone
by choice.

Twelve hundred times....
His final bull surprised him
even as he stabbed and left him
crumpled, gored and bleeding
on the sand.

That memory
is ours to swallow like the bread
of sorrow and the wine of contradiction.
It shows that valor's a delaying
action after all.

If done
with grace, we praise the artistry
and skill.

If not, we say
the unexpected is the way
that life can always overrule us
in the name of life.

And life
can spare.

And life can kill.

Monsieur Camus, you gave
  the stone of our absurdity a name.
Daily we roll it to our graves.
There's no reprieve.
                    Regardless,
  you believed we'd never come
  alive until we chose to live
  without appeal for living's
  sake alone.
                  Such choices
  put self-murder in its place.
Later, you wrote that we are best
  when we rebel—against the casual
  unfairness of the world, against
  acceptance and the cowardice
  it hides, against rebellion
  itself.
              Rebelling with your pen,
  you called the evil of our age
  our willingness to kill within
  the law.
              You cited war
  and punishments called capital.
Today you'd add the legal
  murders of the undesirable,
  the old, the differently religious,
  or the merely different and the not
  yet born.
              But why go on?
You wrote as poets write.
You showed our shame to us
  and stopped us like a stroke.

For you real justice meant
  how daringly we face the unavoidable
  while struggling for the unattainable.
Because your words defined
  our century the way a hub
  defines a wheel, I've come
  with other pilgrims here to pay
  my last respects.
                Standing
  beside your name and life-dates
  nicked in rock, I disagree
  with history.
              Your elegists believed
  your sudden death by accident
  near Villeblevin was premature.
If you could speak, you would
  have said that chance makes
  nothing premature, that lifetimes
  never end the way they should....
But what is all this disquisition
  to the life of Lourmarin?
              The flowers
  of the sun return its Cyclops
  stare the way they always have.
Sweet lavender grows wild
  across your grave.
              The vineyards
turn the wind to musk.
              And all
  the never-to-be-duplicated clouds
  look undisturbed and indestructible.

HOW MARRIED PEOPLE ARGUE

Because they disagreed on nuclear
  disarmament, because he'd left
  the grass uncut, because she'd spilled
  a milkshake on his golf bag,
  he raced ten miles faster
  than the limit.
              Stiffening,
  she scowled for him to stop it.
His answer was to rev it up
  to twenty.
            She asked him why
  a man of his intelligence would
  take out his ill-temper on a car?
He shouted in the name of Jesus
  that he never ever lost
  his damn temper.
             She told him
  he was shouting—not to shout—
  that shouting was a sign of no
  intelligence.
            He asked a backseat
  witness totally invisible
  to anyone but him why women
  had to act like this.
            She muttered,
  "Men," as if the word were mouthwash
  she was spitting in a sink.
            Arriving
  at the party, they postponed the lethal
  language they were saving for the kill
  and played 'Happily Married.'
Since all the guests were gorging
  on chilled shrimp, the fake went
  unobserved.

She found a stranger's
jokes so humorous she almost
choked on her martini.
                    He demonstrated
for the hostess how she could
improve her backswing.
                    All the way
home they played "Married
and So What."
                    She frowned as if
the car had a disease.
                    He steered
like a trainee, heeding all
speed limits to the letter,
whistling "Some Enchanted Evening"
in the wrong key, and laughing
in a language only he could
understand.
                    At midnight, back
to back in bed, he touched
the tightness of her thigh.
                    She muttered,
"I'm asleep," as if her permanent address
were sleep.
                    He rose and roamed
the darkened house, slammed
every door he passed and watched
a prison film with George Raft.
Abed at dawn, he heard
the tears she meant for him
to hear.
                    He listened and lay still.
Because they both had round-trip
tickets to the past but only

one-way tickets to the future,
he apologized for both of them.
They waited for their lives to happen.
He said the hostess's perfume
was Eau de Turpentine.
                              She said
the party was a drag—no humor.
Word by word, they wove themselves
in touch again.
                    Then silence
drew them close as a conspiracy
until whatever never was
the issue turned into the nude
duet that settled everything
until the next time.

THE SONG OF THE HORSE

My father said, "All horses
  when they run are beautiful."
I think of that each time
  I watch Arabians in silhouette,
  the clobbering drays, the jet
  stallions that policemen rein,
  the stilting foals and colts, the sometimes
  bumping always pumping rumps
  of geldings harnessed to a rig.
They prance through war and history:
  "Without a horse the Mongols
  never could have conquered Europe."
And tragedy: "A horse, a horse,
  my kingdom for a horse!"
And sport: "Five minutes
  of hard polo will exhaust
  the strongest horse on earth."
Unsaddled and afoot, how far
  could Cossack, cowboy, Indian,
  and cavalier have gone?
                    What made
  so many generals and emperors
  prefer their portraiture on horseback?
What simulacrum but a horse
  succeeded where Achilles failed?
And where did John put hatred,
  famine, pestilence and war
  but on the backs of horses?
                    And that's
  not all.
          Pegasus still says
to gravity that poetry's none
other than a horse with wings.

It's not a question of intelligence.
Horses, like poetry, are not
   intelligent—just perfect
   in a way that baffles conquest,
   drama, polo, plow,
   and shoe.
               So poem-perfect
   that a single fracture means
   a long, slow dying in the hills
   or, if man's around, the merciful
   aim an inch below the ear.
But when they run, they make
   the charge of any boar at bay,
   the prowl of all the jungle
   cats, the tracking beagle,
   or the antelope in panic seem
   ignoble.
               Just for the sake
   of the running, the running, the running
   they run....
               And not another
   animal on two or four
   or forty legs can match
   that quivering of cords beneath
   their pelts, the fury in their manes,
   the hooves that thump like rapid
   mallets on the earth's mute drum,
   the exultation of the canter and the gallop
   and the rollick and frolic and the jump.

Whatever you can buy's not valuable
  enough, regardless of the cost.
What can't be bought's invaluable.
Not just the white freedom
  of a rose, sparrows in their soaring
  circuses, that girl from Amsterdam
  so tanly tall in Montfleury,
  harbors at noon with clouds
  above them pillowing like snow
  and absolutely still.
                      I'm talking
love.
      I'm talking love
and poetry and everything that's true
of each and interchangeably of both.
Randomly free, they leave
  us grateful to no giver
  we can name.
                They prove what cannot
  last can last forever even
  when we say it's lost....
Some losers ache like Aengus
  or like Leila's madman, pining
  for a time so briefly given
  and so quickly gone.
               Bereft,
  they raise their anguish into songs
  that give a tongue to wounds
  that never heal.
             In every song
  they imitate those troubadours
  whose poems have outlived
  their lives.

Forget how far
they went in school, their ages
or their kin.
              Whatever wanted
to be said and wanted only them
to say it made them what
they are.
              It turned them
into words that we can share
like bread and turn into ourselves.
They asked, as I am asking now,
  for some less unforgiving way
  to say it, and there isn't.
Or if what happened once
  might be repeated, and it can't.
Or if another poet's words
  would say it better, and they don't.
Or if this cup could pass
  and spare them poetry and all
  its contradictions, and it won't.

No one but you could write,
  "Our Father Who art in Heaven
  can lick their Father Who art
  in Heaven."
              After we laughed,
we saw all wars from Troy
to Vietnam in those two lines.
You had the gift of turning
  smiles into thoughts in such
  a quiet, Quaker way.
              And yet
  the saying stayed so casual
  and conversational and untranslatably
Bill Stafford.
            I still remember
when we read in Michigan
together—you from a spiral
notebook crammed with short
poems in longhand.
             Listening,
  I strove to spot where the poems
  stopped, and the prose began.
I never found the seam....
When you wrote *Someday, Maybe*
  what was it you were telling us?
If it was loss, that day
  was yesterday.
             You finished polishing
  a poem that would be your last,
  stood up to help your wife,
  and fell like a soldier.
            As endings
go, that seems regrettably
acceptable.

But why does it
remind me of the silence following
a poem's final line?
I want the poem to go on
forever, but it doesn't.
                             And it does.

UNDERSTORY

It's not that sometimes I forget.
I'm told that everybody does.
What troubles me is how
   whatever I've forgotten trebles
   in importance the more I keep
   forgetting it.
                  Some word....
                        Some place....
Today a student from the Class
   of Way Back When
   seemed certain I'd remember him
   by name.
              I tried and tried
   before I had to ask....
                        Though students
   and ex-students are my life,
   I must admit that I remember
   most of the best, all
   of the worst, many who have left
   this world and not that many
   of the rest.
              It leaves me wondering....
Is memory a beast that sheds
   its baggage as it goes?
Are facts by definition destined
   for oblivion?
                  Or is it absolute
   that what I can't forget no matter
   how I try is all that's worth
   remembering?
                  I know a mother
   of four sons who mixes up
   their names.

94

                    Ollie is Bennett.
Bennett is Drew.
                    Drew
is Christopher.
                    Facing one,
she'll travel down the list before
she'll ask, "Tell me your name,
dear boy."
                    Outsiders realize
they're all one boy to her,
regardless of their names.
                                    She knows
them by their souls.
                    That reassures me.

For JoAnn Bevilacqua-Weiss

The swing's unslung and winter-waxed,
   the mint leaves waiting to be sieved
   to salt, the hose unscrewed
   and coiled like a rattler in the shed.
As usual the ripening figs
   will blacken at first frost
   exactly as they did last year
   when all the talk was war.
This year the human harvest
   makes the war seem dim:
   one suicide, three deaths, one
   shock, one disappointment, and a swindle.
Each one bequeathed its epitaph:
   "Your letter was a narrow bridge
   to the rest of my life."
                              "He didn't
   recognize me, Sam—his own
   sister."
               "I'll stay until he's well
   or else not here anymore."
Remembering, I see how much
   can never be the way it was,
   despite appearances.
                              Philosophy's
   no help.
               Religion's even less.
And poetry does nothing but re-live
   what's lost without redeeming it
   like life's exact revenge
   upon itself.
               What's left
   but learning to survive with wounds?

Or studying the fate of figs
  before the unexpected chill,
  not knowing in advance how many
  or how few will be destroyed
  or toughened when it comes...
Playing for time, I occupy
  myself with chores and tools,
  uncertain if the lot I've chosen
  is a gambler's or a coward's or a fool's.

You think of photographic paper
  drowning in developer.
                            Slowly
  the whiteness darkens into forms.
Shadows become a face;
  the face, a memory; the memory,
  a name.
             The final clari2ty
  evolves without a rush
  until it's there.
               It's like
  your struggle to remember
  what you know you know
  but just can't quite recall.
No matter how you frown,
  the secret stays beyond you.
You reach.
          It moves.
                  You reach
  again.
          Again it moves.
It's disobedience itself, but still
  it wants so much to be regained
  by you, only by you.
                  Later,
  when it lets itself be known,
  you wonder how you ever could
  have lost so obvious a thing.
And yet you take no credit
  for retrieving it.
              It came to you
  on its own terms, at its
  own time.

You woke, and it
was there like love or luck
or life itself and asked
no more of you than knowing
it by name.
                    The name is yours
to keep.
            You burn to share
this sudden and surprising gold
with everyone.
                    You feel the glee
of being unexpectedly complete
and sure and satisfied and chosen.

The darkening space in my projectile
   lightens with the voice of a great
   poet speaking his Swedish
   poems in English.
                          In fact
   he's speechless, strangled by a stroke
   so that the only voice
   that's his is this one on a tape....
I see him blanketed near Stockholm,
   waiting for Monica, thinking
   of midsummer in the archipelago.
If dreams were words, I'd tell
   this man how much I need
   his poems and how true they are.
They heal like sacraments.
                          Instead,
   I watch the road before me
   change into the road behind me
   like a threat faced once and then
   forgotten.
                 The poems fill
   the car like Schubert at his best.
They guide me like a compass
   to a home far truer
   than the one I'm heading for.
Which takes more bravery—to live
   with words that never can be said
   or steer through Pennsylvania
   darkness in the rain?
                          "His humor
   is wonderful, so we are more close
   than ever."

These words were Monica's
last year, and I repeat them
to the darkness, word by word.
Meanwhile, the tape reverses,
    and I let it play.
                    The compass
steadies to a truer north
than north.
                    It says that "patience
is love at rest," and love
means everything.
                    Beside such certitude
I seem a man without virtue.

My father said, "Your work
    is never over—always
    one more page."
                    This
    from a traveling man whose life
    was always one more mile.
I told him that.
                    "Sometimes
    I hate the road," he said,
    "it's made me so I'm never
    happy in one place.
                    Don't
    you get started."
                    I never did,
    spending my days at universities,
    my nights at home.
                    Not
    typically the academic, not
    totally at home at home,
    I think of how I could have lived
    and come up blank.
                    What's
    better than sharing all you know
    and all you don't with students
    who do just the same?
                    Even
    on the worst of days it justifies
    the time.
            Or inking out
    your real future on white
    paper with a fountain pen
    and listening to what the writing
    teaches you?

          Compared to walking
on the moon or curing polio,
it seems so ordinary.
                  And it is.
But isn't living ordinary?
For two and fifty summers
  Shakespeare lived a life
so ordinary that few scholars
  deal with it.
             And what of Faulkner
down in ordinary Oxford, Mississippi?
Or Dickinson, the great recluse?
Or E. B. White, the writer's
  writer?
          Nothing extraordinary
there, but, God! what wouldn't
we give for one more page?

AT THE SITE OF THE MEMORIAL

1

No soldiers choose to die.
It's what they risk by being
    who and where they are.
It's what they dare while saving
    someone else whose life means
    suddenly as much to them
    as theirs.
                    Or more.
                                    To honor them
why speak of duty or the will
of governments?
                                    Think first of love
each time you tell their story.
It gives their sacrifice a name
    and takes from war its glory.

2

Seeing my words in stone
    reminds me of a grave....
Not that the words are wrong,
    but seeing them so permanent
    makes me feel posthumous as those
    commemorated here.
                                    Lawson,
    Gideon, Butler, Pinder,
    Port, Sarnoski, Shughart....

Stephanie Shughart tells me,
   "Randy and I had twenty-two
months."
            She smiles as if
to prove that gratitude and grief
can be compatible.
                  I want
to believe her....
            Brady, who saved
5,000 men by Medivac
and lived, reads every dead
man's name as if it were
his own.
            He'll read them in his dreams.
Next to the next of kin,
   I think how all these men
risked everything for something
more than living on.
                  Life meant
not one more day for them
but one more act.
                  Just one....

Some say they just reflect "the nightly
   love of the sea and the moon."
But life and physiology have never
   rhymed.
              Think of the squat
queen who tranced Marc Antony
and Caesar with her glances to become
all Egypt to them both.
                         Or dancers
who have spines like spears
and walk as if mere walking
were a dance.
                Or nurses in their
white, sure, soft
shoes, nimble as prancers
in motion and just as self-possessed.
Such poise and prowess are the stuff
   of mystery.
              And mystery it is.
What else but mystery imbues
a woman of stature to subdue
a mob with nothing but a stance
or stare?
          Or tells why men
or countrymen can languish
with their goddess gone?
                         Learning
of Piaf's death, Cocteau decided
not to live.
              For what?
                         For a lifelong
waif whose voice was France
for half a century.

And what
of Om Khalsoum who stilled
the Arab world each time she sang
and drew four million (four
million!) to her funeral?
                    Or Marilyn
Monroe whose public grows
and grows?
                    Is this bewitchery?
Or is it something that will never
have a name?
                    Or does it simply
mean that women live within
their bodies to the end—and past
the end?
                    Not so for men
who seem to leave their bodies
as they age, regarding what was once
an instrument as now a thing
of no or little use.
                    For those
whose destination is themselves,
what are such losses but a nuisance,
not a destiny?
                    Compared to love
or happiness or children, they appear
at best as vanities.
                    See
for yourselves.
                    The eyes of any
woman say it takes more bravery
to be and bear than to beget.
Or finally just be, with no
defenses, no illusions, no regrets.

Watching two lives converge
   through all your predecessors down
   the centuries to you is miracle
   enough.
                  But all that is
   is history.
                     You're more than that.
If choosing is the most that freedom
   means, you're free.
                        If choosing
   one you love for life
   is freedom at its best,
   you're at your best today.
No wonder we're exuberant.
Today's become an instant
   anniversary for all of us.
You've brought us back to what's
   the most important choice
   of all.
                  You've shown that where
   we come from matters less
   than who we are, and who
   we are is what we choose
   to be....
                  We're all familiar
   with the risks.
                        No matter how
   or whom we love, we know
   we're each on loan to one
   another for a time.
                        We know
   we're God's employees picked

for unforeseen assignments
we'll be given on the way.
                    The secret
is to love until the summoning,
regardless of the odds....
                    Go now
together in the unison of mates.
Go happily with all our hopes
and all our blessings.
                    And with God's.

For Sam and Dawn

> "If you can see your path laid out ahead of you
> step by step, then you know it's not your path."
> *Joseph Campbell*

Inside Brooks Brothers' windows
    it's July.
            Sportshirts on sleek
dummies speak in turquoise,
polo, Bermuda and golf.
Outside, it's very much the first
    of March.
                The sportshirts say
today's tomorrow and the present
tense be damned.
                They tell me
to forget that here's the only place
we have.
                They claim what matters
most is never now but next.
I've heard this argument before.
It leaves me sentenced to the future,
    and that's much worse than being
    sentenced to the past.
                        The past
at least was real just once....
                        What's
called religion offers me the same.
Life's never what we have
    but what's to come.
                        But where
    did Christ give heaven its address
    except within each one of us?
So, anyone who claims it's not
    within but still ahead is contradicting
    God.

But why go on?
I'm sick of learning to anticipate.
I never want to live a second
   or a season or a heaven in advance
   of when I am and where.
I need the salt and pepper
   of uncertainty to know I'm still
alive.
        It makes me hunger
   for the feast I call today.
It lets desire keep what
   satisfaction ends.
           Lovers
remember that the way that smoke
remembers fire.
          Between anticipation
and the aggravation of suspense, I choose
suspense.
        I choose desire.

Her letter, mailed from Saranac,
  is dated 1926.
                    My mother's
writing to my aunt.
                    It's two
years since she told her father,
"Dad, I'm marrying Sam
and not the man you had
in mind."
            That's decades more
  than half a century ago.
My mother and my aunt are dead.
I'm well past sixty when I share
  my mother's letter with my wife.
It stills us like a resurrection.
Later I read it to my son
  and to his wife.
                    They tell me
  how alive it seems as if
a woman neither ever knew
is speaking in this very room
to each of us.
                    The letter's full
of questions I can answer,
  but the time for answering is over.
I realize my life's already longer
  than my mother's was by almost
thirty years.
                    The letter in my hand
  is older than the two of us.
The more I read, the less
  there is to read until

I reach the bottom of the page.
The last sentence ends
  with a hyphen.
                There's no page two.

Nothing was surer amid all the furor
than watching a stock that I picked on a hunch
make rich men of paupers, and paupers of fools,
and all in the pinch that it took to eat lunch.

My betting and cheering took real engineering.
I guessed and I gauged and I bet and I prayed
from the dawn of the bull to the dusk of the bear
where fortunes were waiting and fortunes were made.

The world of percents is a world that resents
whenever its buyouts are less than a steal.
Its language is numbers, and numbers are lethal,
and all that makes sense is the luck of the deal.

You have to like poker to be a good broker.
You have to take chances and hope for the best.
Buy cheap and sell dear is the law of the market,
and woe unto those who forget or protest.

Like any good broker I loved to play poker,
but poker's a gamble where all that you've got
is the lure of the cards and the stack of the chips
and the dice of the draw and the pay of the pot....

I took all my winnings that some called my sinnings,
and lived like a king where the snow never fell.
I drank all my juices and swallowed my pills,
and bet on the races, and down came hell....

It cost me my wife in the prime of my life.
It made me content with much less than the best.
I worked for the day when I never would work,
and the money was sure, and the honey was rest.

If you'd rather be healthy than feeble and wealthy...
if you'd rather be happy than wed to a bed,
then think of a man with a millionaire's tan
who died half a lifetime before he was dead.

SEPTEMBER 11, 2001

1

The hawk seems almost napping
  in his glide.
          His arcs are perfect
as geometry.
          His eyes hunger
for something about to panic,
something small and unaware.
Higher by six thousand feet
  an airbus vectors for its port,
  its winglights aiming dead
ahead like eyesight.
          The natural
and scheduled worlds keep happening
according to their rules....
          "We interrupt
this program...."
          Inch by inch
the interruption overrules both worlds,
engulfing us like dustfall
from a building in collapse.
          The day
turns dark as an eclipse.
          We head
for home as if to be assured
that home is where we left it.

2

Before both towers drowned
  in their own dust, someone
  downfloated from the hundredth floor.

Then there were others—plunging,
  stepping off or diving in tandem,
  hand in hand, as if the sea
  or nets awaited them.
                        "My God,
  people are jumping!"
                       Of all
  the thousands there, we saw
  those few, just those, freefalling
  through the sky like flotsam from a blaze....
Nightmares of impact crushed us.
We slept like the doomed or drowned,
  then woke to oratory, vigils,
  valor, journalists declaring war
  and, snapping from aerials or poles,
  the furious clamor of flags.

He knew he was older and taller.
He saw that the towns were the same.
What made them seem suddenly smaller?
What made him feel somehow to blame

for all that was done to a village
to save a surrounded platoon?
The huts were just booty to pillage
on a hillscape as spare as the moon.

A man with one leg saw him walking
and offered him tea on a mat.
They spent the whole afternoon talking
while his wife cooked the head of a cat.

It wasn't his squad he remembered.
It wasn't the sergeant at Hue
who found his lieutenant dismembered
and buried him there where he lay.

What troubled him most were the places
that once were just places to fight.
He thought of the nightfighters' faces
all blackened to blend with the night.

The whores in their teens were forgotten
and gone were their overnight dates,
and grown were the idly begotten
whose fathers were back in the States.

He never regretted returning.
At least he had lessened his dread.
But the toll that it took for the learning
was 58,000 dead.

He walked in a daze near the water.
He sat all alone on the shore
like a man making peace with the slaughter,
though the price for this peace was war.

What's welcome is your French disdain
  of dogma.
             Quotations from Solon,
  Horace, Virgil and Plato,
  of course....
           Digressions on food,
  ambition and fatherhood, assuredly....
But all in the spirit of conversation—
  without an angle, so to speak.
When you call marriage a "discreet
  and conscientious voluptuousness,"
  I partially agree.
             After
  you explain that "valor" and "value"
  are etymologically akin, I see
  the connection.
           Nothing seems
  contentious.
            Your views on cruelty
  recall Tertullian's platitude
  that men fear torture more than death.
Of honors you are tolerant, noting
  that honors are most esteemed
  when rare and quoting Martial
  in support: "To him who thinks
  none bad, whoever can seem good?"
If mere consistency identifies
  small minds, you never were small.
One incident explains: perpetuating
  family names you called a vanity,
  and yet you willed your name
  and fortune to your daughter's
  youngest son.

Since she was married
twice and had two families,
two hundred years of litigation
followed.
Why?
Because
Montaigne the grandpère silenced
Montaigne the philosopher, which proves
once more that irony, not reason,
rules the blood.
Otherwise,
your breadth of thought amazes me.
Each meal's a feast whose menu
is the universe.
So here's a toast,
my friend, across four centuries.
To essays that seem to write
themselves and sound like tabletalk.
To hospitality of mind where nothing
is immune from scrutiny.
To all
that leaves me wisely confused
but even in confusion, wiser.

A dozen mallards squawk
  in a shortarm vee above
  Lake Huron.
                Without a physicist
  among them, they slip each other's
  jetwash and wing northward
  equidistantly at cloud-speed.
I put aside the wartime prose
  of Antoine de St.-Exupéry
  and track the ducks to Canada.
To be dull as a duck aground
  but awesome in flight and even
  more awesome in print describes
  St.-Ex in life and death.
If poetry is prose that soars,
  his prose in fact is poetry.
It made Consuelo overlook
  his dalliances, his sleight-of-hand
  with cards, his sudden absences.
How many men dare gravity
  with wings and words and win
  as no one did before
  or since?
                Meanwhile,
  over the rhythm of waves
  the mallards are rowing the wind
  in perfect rhyme to show
  what's possible without instruction.

BREAKDOWN

Like soldiers ordered to "Fall in,"
  platoons of starlings swoop
and muster on a telephone line.
Equidistant and at birds' attention,
  they mimic ranks at "Parade Rest."
Suddenly they dive into the air
  on cue, swirling in a bluster
of wings like a dream gone mad.
For just that long, I think
  that madness rules the world,
  despite appearances.
                    "Change
the rhythm," Pindar predicted,
"and the walls of the city will fall."
It takes so little....
                  Vary
the height and width of any step
by just a fraction, and the rhythm
of a stairway dies.
                  Change
traffic patterns, and we slacken
to the speed of doubt.
                    Or let
come war, and we're undone
as if the sea breathed in
and never out against our shores,
surrounding, pounding, drowning
everything.
                It imitates what happens
when I'm writing, and the words
won't perch.

They swirl confused
as any flock in flight.
They're swirling
now.
I'm losing touch
with what I should be saying,
and I can't remember what I think
I meant.
The tempo's gone
completely....
Pindar was right.

Be they belaureled as the king
   of cats, I'll not recant.
Euphues is no more poet
   than a pig, oinking his drivel
   at the moon.
                         And singsong rhymers
   by the millions shrink to nil
   beside the singer of the "Song
of Songs."
                     Nor does allegiance
   to a master-piper matter
   in the least.
                     Name one of all
   the acolytes who formed the Tribe
of Ben.
                  Lovers of a sort
   may toast the aromatic meat
   of wenches, but their rhapsodies
   at midnight disappear by dawn.
And those who pen for pelf
   and hawk their words as marketeers
   deserve the wages of disdain.
The time of breath is much
   too brief for humbug.
                               Let us
   have poetry that strikes us dumb
   or leaves us stabbed so deeply
   that the wound in perpetuity stays raw.
Let us have that or nothing.

Great sailors though they were,
  the Greeks abhorred the sea.
What was it but a gray
  monotony of waves, wetness
  in depth, an element by nature
  voyager-unfriendly and capricious?
Sailing in sight of shore,
  they always beached at night
  to sleep before the next day's
  rowing.
         Taming the sea
  by beating it with rods
  they named the ultimate insanity—
  a metaphor too obvious to paraphrase.
In short, they knew a widow-
  maker when they saw one.
             Still,
  for honor, commerce or a kidnapped
  queen, they waged their lives
  against what Homer called wine-dark
  and deep.
         Some came back never.
Some learned too late that pacing
  a deck was far less hazardous
  than facing what awaited them
  at home....
         Homer would praise
  their iliads and odysseys in song.
Aeschylus, Euripides and Sophocles
  would watch and wait, then write
  of wars much closer to the heart.

They knew the lives of men—
  no matter how adventurous—
  would end as comedies or tragedies.
They wrote that both were fundamentally
  and finally domestic.
                      Homer
could sing his fill.
                  The dramatists
dared otherwise.
                Compared
to troubles in a family, they saw
this business with the sea and swords—
regardless of the risk—as minor.

The sculpted head of Gustave V
  scowls at a sundial park
  near the Place Massena.
                              Benches
  circle the dial.
                    On one
  a woman in a walking cast
  rests her bandaged ankle
  on a package.
                    On the next a man
  with a gray pigtail is arguing
  in angry German on a cellphone.
Cohesively chattering Japanese
  flock by.
              The last one
  in the flock's a boy outfitted
  in a New York Yankees
  uniform.
                  He tries and tries
  again to coax a French
  pigeon closer with a crumb.
Strutting off like a Japanese
  general, the pigeon gargles
  and ululates in pigeonese.
From the last bench I watch
  this random comedy of characters
  ad-libbing in performance as they pass.
I'm here because I never
  drowned in Watertown, had orders
  to Lejeune and not Korea,
  was spared the last and lethal
  stings of mudwasps on a rampage,
  missed the jet that plummeted
  in Hopewell.

Common, unremarkable
reprieves have given me
this afternoon in Nice like someone
left unchosen from a lottery.
I watch.
    I realize how much
depends on chance.
        I recognize
the reckless amnesty of God.

In Arabic a single word
  describes the very act
  of taking a position.
                          Greeks
  pronounce three syllables
  to signify the sense of doom
  that all Greeks fear when things
  are going very well.
                          As for
  the shameful ease we feel
  when bad news happens
  to someone else, including
  friends?
                  In Greek—one word.
To designate the hose that funnels
  liquid fire down the turret
  of a tank in battle, the Germans
  speak one word.
                          It's three
  lines long but still one word.
And as for John, Matthew,
  Mark and Luke?
                          There's not
  a surname in the lot.
                          With just
  one name they match in memory
  the immortality of martyrs.
                          The longer
  they're dead, the more they live….
I praise whatever mates
  perception with precision!

                        It asks
us only to be spare and make
the most of least.
                        It simplifies
and lets each word sound final
as a car door being shut
but perfect as a telegram to God.

I thought of women basically
  as fruit: delectable when ripe,
  dismissible past prime,
  disposable when old.
                        I'm not
to blame.
               You made young women
irresistible, not I.
                  My sin—
if it was sin at all—was ultimate
enjoyment of Your handiwork.
That girl from Padua—the supple
  once-ness of her kiss....
                    Her cousin
from Trieste—the way her breasts
  announced themselves....
                  Surely
You appreciate the patience and the skill
it takes to bring a virgin
  to the point where shame means nothing.
I'm not a rapist, after all.
The ones I chose were single,
  willing, totally agreeable.
They wanted to be loved deliciously.
Not roughly like those toughs who pinched
  them in the street, but step
  by gentle step and never in a hurry.
First, some conversation.
               Then,
  a kiss on either cheek.
Then everything that You alone
  could see: a jettison of clothes,

my palm along her inner thigh,
our loins in juncture as we hugged,
the mounting puffs and shudders
on the sheets, the parting, the repose.
It made me marvel at the way
    You fashioned us for mating
face to face—essentially
two kinds of kissing happening
in one position all at once.
Because I reached perfection in the act,
    some called me a philanderer....
Pronounce me guilty if You like....
I'm reconciled.
                    I did what I
alone could do when I could
do it.
            Who says desire dies?
Today I'm tended by a nurse
    who spoons me noodles from a cup.
She tells me to relax.
                    Relax?
When a woman naked underneath
    her whites and silks is just a breath
away from Giacomo Girolamo
Casanova of Venice?
                    Impossible.

Who was it wrote, "If women
  had mustaches, they would somehow
  make them beautiful.

                   Look
what they've done with breasts!"
Who disagrees?

                  Doesn't the Bible
say a woman just an inch
from death will keep an eye
for color?

              And don't philosophers
agree that women sacrifice
the ultimate on beauty's altar?
And love's?

             Why scoff at that?
Are the male gods of money,
  fame and power more deserving?
What's money but guilt?

                What's fame
but knowing people you will never
know will know your name?
What's power but pride translated
  into force?

             Are these worth more
than what sustains us to the end?
Consider Bertha.

            Eighty, blind
and diabetic, she believed that death's
real name was Harold.

             "I want
to know what Harold has to offer,"
she would say.

She'd seen
her children's children's children
and presumed she had a poet's right
to give a name to death, if so
she chose.
　　　Chuckling to herself,
she watched and waited for this last
adventure in her life....
　　　　Then
there was Jane, who mothered seven
and left unfinished all her art
by choice as if to prove
that incompleteness is the rule
of life where nothing ends
the way it should...or when.
Two weeks before her funeral
she called all seven to her bed
to say, "I hope to see you all
again...but not right away...."
So here's to the honor of Bertha,
and here's to the glory of Jane!
Let them be spoken of wherever
beauty's lovers gather to applaud
the beauty of love.
　　　　Let them
not rest in peace but thrive
in everlasting action, doing
what they love the most.
　　　　Who wants
a heaven that's equivalent to one
long sleep?

Those crypted, supine
saints in their basilicas can keep
the dream of their Jerusalem.
                              The soul
was meant for more than that.
Pray for us, St. Bertha.
Pray for us, St. Jane.

"Have you ever looked into a flower, Mr. Gable?"
Grace Kelly

Look in, and the flower stares back.
Its iris offers you the very
  whites, blues, pinks
  and lavenders of God.
                    Each petal
  revels in the final glory
  of itself.
          For those distracted
  by horizons I propose five minutes
  in the company of tulips.
                    One
  tulip will suffice in all
  its purple understatement.
                    Look deep
  and see what's primping to its prime
  before it fades and falls,
  and you'll be mesmerized for life.
Brides in their wedding veils
  would understand.
                    They know
  it's not duration but expression
  that survives our days.
                    They flower
  in their one-time gowns
  just once for just one day.
Even though it ends, it stays.

"Your body's slowed down, my dearest dear.
Your body's slowed down, my dearest."
"I'm aging, my dear—just aging, I fear.
Each day I keep growing older....
The birds in the trees may never freeze,
but the blood as you age grows colder."

"Remember the days when we used to play
and hug on the sheets of the bed there?
You'd touch me here and touch me here,
and then we would wrestle together?
Instead we lie now like the dead there
and listen all night to the weather."

"Remember the money we managed to save
and planned to enjoy in our sixties?
Well, sixty has come, and sixty has gone,
and what have our savings returned us
but travel in season without a good reason
and tropical sunlight that burned us?"

"Remember the friends we knew, we knew,
when we and our friends were younger?
Where have they gone, and why don't they write,
and why have the decades divided
all those not alive from those who survive
no matter how well they're provided?"

"But why blame our fears on the innocent years?
They're gone and beyond re-living.
Since death's quite efficient, and time's insufficient,

is it asking too much to forgive us
for wanting to stay till the end of the day
and love what the years can still give us?"

"So give me a kiss, my dearest of dears,
and sleep by my side forever.
Let the years come, and let the years go.
We treasure what nothing can sever.
In touch or apart is the same to the heart.
Until death parts us not, we're together."

It lasts like a parade in place
  with only the essentials cut
  in rhyming white headstones:
  last names, initials,
  rank, branches of service.
The names answer up in a muster
  of silence while Washington's a-glut
  with traffic, vectoring jets
  and disproportion.
                        Maple groves,
  road signs and gardens
  remember Lady Bird and LBJ.
Facing the Department of Commerce,
  Reagan's billion-dollar
  palace rivals in square
  feet the whole damn Pentagon.
Roosevelt's granite marker,
  scaled as he asked to the length
  and width of his desk, is harder
  to find.
              Jack Kennedy,
  his widow, two children
  and his brother share one plot.
Across the slow Potomac,
  the names in black marble
  of 58,000 futile deaths
  consecrate less than an acre.

My left leg was gone with the boot still on—
the boot that I laced in the morning.
I felt like a boy who had stepped on a toy
and made it explode without warning.

They choppered me back to a medical shack
with no one but corpsmen to heed me.
I stared at the sky and prayed I would die,
and I cursed when the nurse came to feed me.

I knew that I must, so I tried to adjust
while orderlies struggled to teach me
the will of the crutch and the skill of the cane
and assured me their methods would reach me.

The President came with his generals tame
and explained why he never relieved us.
But the red, white and blue of my lone, right shoe
told the world how he lied and deceived us.

They buried my shin and my bones and my skin
an ocean away from this writing.
But pain finds a way on each given day
to take me straight back to the fighting

when I served with the Corps in a slaughterhouse war
where we tallied our killings like cattle,
as if these explain why the armies of Cain
behave as they do in a battle....

Whatever's a bore, you can learn to ignore,
but a leg's not a limb you like leaving.
So you deal with regret and attempt to forget
what always is there for the grieving.

If you look for a clue while I stand in a queue,
you can't tell what's real from prosthetic.
I walk with a dip that begins at my hip,
but I keep it discreet and aesthetic.

If you're ordered on line and step on a mine,
you learn what it means to be only
a name on a chart with a hook in your heart
and a life that turns suddenly lonely.

Lose arms, and you're left incomplete and bereft.
Lose legs, and you're fit for a litter.
Lose one at the knee, and you're just like me
with night after night to be bitter.

For Ray Fagan

Immortality?
         Too general a concept.
Some say it's never-ending time,
   which means it's long on myth
   and short on meaning.
                  Some say
   it's never to be known until
   it's ours.
            Some say, some say....
I stand with those who think
   it could be quick as any instant
   going on and on and on
   within itself like poetry or music
   or a kiss.
         That comes as close
   as anything to God's, "I am
   Who am."
            No past.
                     No memory.
No future but the time at hand
   that's passing even as it's born....
Once I was driving due southeast
   through Pennsylvania.
                  Highways
   were broad and dangerous and everyone's.
As I ran out of Pennsylvania,
   farm by farm, I noticed
   border signs that welcomed me
   to Maryland where Rand McNally
   said that Maryland began.
I knew the earth was still
   the earth in Maryland or Pennsylvania.

I knew I stayed the same,
  border or no border....
                    From here
  into hereafter could be just
  like that—our selfsame selves
  translated instantly from state
  to state to God alone
  knows what....
                    That's immortality.

Leaves curl against the ground
  like Muslims at prayer.
                    In weeks
  they'll change from elegies in place
  into their own obituaries.
                    Now
  they leave me leafing back,
  back, back.
                    My father meets me
  on the way.
                    At eighty he told me
  he was shrinking.
                    Lately, I've felt
  the same, not physically, but otherwise.
The more I add the sum of all
  the living to the once alive,
  the more I seem to vanish
  in the balance.
                    Watching the way
  of leaves prefigures what I know
  will come.
                    It makes me want
  to board a ship called Elsewhere
  or name my house Defiance.
Instead I choose to mount
  my mutiny in words....
                    Not much
  as protests go, but something.

I keep whatever stays as intimate
  as breath and, like all breathing,
  of the instant: my father's aftershave,
  the whiteness of his shirts, his hair
  still black at eighty-two,
  the hats he always wore brim up,
  the eyes of Cynthia gone sullen
  with desire, supper in Geneva
  when a waiter in tuxedo boned
  the lemon sole as deftly as a surgeon
  operating on an eye, the day
  of Kennedy's murder when all
  the clocks struck nil and stayed there,
  my last goodbye to Jane
  and how we sensed it as we spoke.
Compared to these, who cares
  if Candidate Twice and Candidate Once
  insult the day with presidential
  dreams?
        For them today's
a preface, nothing more.
             The same
holds true for all who bet
on dynasties, prognostications, jackpots
or the gold of fools.
          I trust
the body's unforgettable assurances
that know what's true without
discussion or hypocrisy.
           The teeth
with just one bite can tell
an apple from a pear.

     The tongue
can savor at a touch what's salt,
what's sugar.
      Balsam and skunk
cannot confuse the nose.
Even in darkness the hand
knows silk from gabardine.
Whatever makes a sound and what
resounds when sound evaporates
is music to the ear.
      The eye
does not discriminate, and everything
in its complete democracy is ours
in perpetuity to keep as near
as here and dearer than now.

THE KISS

While the river turned and slid
  under a gray bridge that cars
  kept crossing on their way
  to Michigan, and somewhere a band
  was blaring a march by Sousa,
  she eased her lips around
  his lips so firmly that the musk
  that rises in the body of a girl
  aroused was his to taste.
In time, when she no longer
  was the mystery for him she used
  to be, the echo of the ichor
  of that kiss could resurrect the grayness
  of the bridge, the spurting cars,
  the river and the drums of Sousa,
  and then, arising like a swimmer
  from the depth of half a century,
  the very face and figure
  of a girl whose mouth sealed his
  so tightly that their top-teeth ticked
  like a kiss gone bumpy
  though the kiss went on and on,
  and when it stopped, the band
  had marched to sleep, the bridge
  was empty and the sliding river
  sailored south without a sound.

1

Everywhere the same campus trees—
  fifty autumns thicker, taller
  and scheduled to sleeve their naked
  bark in January's ermine.
A male and female cardinal
  peck at huckleberries on a limb.
Paired for life, they beak
  each berry as their last and first.
Sparrows cling to branches,
  wires, sheer brick walls,
  anything where they can roost.
A chipmunk scoots and pauses
  by the numbers.
                  Unlike all peacock
  prancers on parade or the zombie
  stomp of soldiery, backpacking
  students cycle, rollerblade
  and stroll to their different drummers.
They pass like Giacometti's
  striders—eyes full front
  but aimed at destinations still
  within themselves....
                Beyond
  Nantucket a jet's about to crash.
Bradley's challenging Gore.
Ted Hesburgh's fit and eighty-two
  with one good eye.
               "May I
  serve God better with one eye
  than I did with two."
               Seated
  behind me at a football game,
  a woman from Dallas tells me

her Pittsburgh mother had an uncle—
Leo O'Donnell, a doctor.
                          She knows
I've flown from Pittsburgh for the day.
Eighty thousand cheer around us.
  "O'Donnell," she repeats.
                            I swallow
and say that Dr. O'Donnell funded
"my scholarship to study here"
a half-century back.
                      The odds
are eighty thousand plus to one
that I should meet his Texas niece
today in this crammed stadium
in Indiana, but I do.
                     What else
is there to say?
               It's now
all over the world.
                  Everything's
happening.
              Anything can happen.

2

We've journeyed back to grass
  and souvenirs and beige bricks.
The sky's exactly the same.
Acre by acre, the campus
  widens like a stage designed
  for a new play.
              Why
do we gawk like foreigners
at residence halls no longer

ours but somehow ours
in perpetuity?
                    We visit them
like their alumni—older
but unchanged.
                        Half a century
of students intervenes.
                            They stroll
among us now, invisible
but present as the air before
they fade and disappear.
                        It's like
the day we swam St. Joseph's
Lake.
            We churned the surface
into suds with every stroke and kick.
After we crossed, the water
    stilled and settled to a sheen
    as if we never swam at all.
One memory was all we kept
    to prove we'd been together
    in that very lake, and swimming.
Each time we tell this story,
    someone says we're living out
    a dream.
                    We say we're only
reuniting with the lives
we lived.
                    As long as we
can say they were, they were....
And what they were, we are.

Conventioneers from thirty-seven
  countries throng the banquet
  hall to hear the message.
A clergyman tells God to bless
  the fruit and rolls.
                 The President
speaks up for Reagan, Martin
Luther King and having faith
in faith.
           Love is the common
theme, most of it touching,
all of it frank, unburdening
and lengthy.
             If faith is saying so,
then this is faith.
              The problem is
that I must be the problem.
I've always thought that faith
  declaimed too publicly destroys
  the mystery.
           Years back,
when Brother Antoninus yelled
at listeners to hear the voice
of Jesus in them, Maura said,
"The Jesus in me doesn't talk
that way."
          Later, when I saw
a placard bannering, "Honk,
if you love Jesus," I thought
of Maura's words and passed
in silence....

Jesus in fact
spoke Aramaic in Jerusalem,
foretold uninterrupted life
and sealed it with a resurrection.
If He asked me to honk
in praise of that, I'd honk
all day.
        But rising from the dead
for me seems honk enough
since no one's done it since,
and no one did it earlier or ever.
Others might disagree, and that's
their right.
        If sounding off
will get them through the night,
the choice is theirs.
                I won't
intrude.
        But there's an inner
voice I hear that's one
on one and never out of date.
It's strongest when it's most subdued.
I'll take my Jesus straight.

5TH Special Basic Class, U. S. Marine Corps

Older by fifty years,
  we grouped for photographs beside
  apartment BOQ's that once
  were Quonset huts.
                 The new
  lieutenants held us in embarrassing
  esteem.
           Of some three hundred
  in our old battalion, three
  were killed in combat, and the rest
  lived on to die of the usual
  or simply to survive and reunite.
Necklaced with tags to prove
  we were who we were, we met
  without bravado.
             Grandfathers mostly,
  we drank black coffee like alumni
  and avoided politics.
            Two days
  together placed us squarely
  in our generation.
           No one pretended
  to be other than himself.
           We parted
  as we parted half a century
  before, uncertain when or where
  we'd meet again.
           Or if.

Alive, she'd be in her nineties.
Dying on Wilkins Avenue
   and buried from home, she never
   saw forty.
                    Six decades back
   I crept downstairs to see her
   coffined in our living room....
Today, through me to my own son
   and through my son to his,
   I'm witness to a resurrection.
                         The baby's
   brows and lashes are hers.
So is the roundness of his face
   and, ever so slightly, the smile....
His mother says he has his father's
   features softened by her.
And I agree.
               But I go further
   back, think long and stop short.
Some things are known at sight,
   some not, and some through memory
   and what the heart can never
   quite deny.
                    And each
   is wrong.
               And both are right.

We thought that the worst was behind us
    in the time of the tumult of nations.
We planned and we saved for the future
    in the time of the tumult of nations.
The crowds in the streets were uneasy
    in the time of the tumult of nations.
We murdered our annual victims
    in the time of the tumult of nations.
We were fined if we smoked in the cities
    in the time of the tumult of nations.
We gave and deducted our givings
    in the time of the tumult of nations.
We kept the bad news from the children
    in the time of the tumult of nations.
We wakened from nightmares with headaches
    in the time of the tumult of nations.
We voted for men we distrusted
    in the time, in the time, in the time,
    in the time of the tumult of nations.

In the time of the tumult of nations
    the ones who were wrong were the loudest.
In the time of the tumult of nations
    the poets were thought to be crazy.
In the time of the tumult of nations
    the President answered no questions.
In the time of the tumult of nations
    protesters were treated like traitors.
In the time of the tumult of nations
    the airports were guarded by soldiers.
In the time of the tumult of nations
    young women kept mace in their purses.
In the time of the tumult of nations
    the rich were exempt in their mansions.

In the time of the tumult of nations
  we waited for trouble to happen.
In the time of the tumult of nations
  we lived for the weekends like children.

Like children we clung to our playthings
  in the time of the tumult of nations.
We huddled in burglar-proof houses
  in the time of the tumult of nations.
We said that the poor had it coming
  in the time of the tumult of nations.
We readied our handguns for trouble
  in the time of the tumult of nations.
We tuned in to war every evening
  in the time of the tumult of nations.
We watched as the bombs burned the cities
  in the time of the tumult of nations.
The name of the game was destruction
  in the time of the tumult of nations.
We knew we were once better people
  in the time of the tumult of nations.
We pretend we are still the same people
  in the time, in the time, in the time,
  in the time of the tumult of nations.

Crosswinds have slashed the flag
  so that the thirteenth ribbon
  dangles free or coils around
  the flagpole like a stripe.
                    What's left
  keeps fluttering in red-and-white
  defiance.
              Somehow the tattering
  seems apropos.
              The President
  proclaims we'll be at war forever—
  not war for peace but war
  upon war, though hopefully not here.
Believers in eternal re-election
  hear his pitch and pay.
                    In Washington
  God's lawyer warns we stand
  at Armageddon, and we battle
  for the Lord.
              Elsewhere, California's
  governor believes in California's
  governor, and football bowls
  are named for Mastercard, Pacific
  Life, Con-Agra and Tostitos.
Out west a plan to gerrymander
  Colorado (Texas-style) fails,
  but barely.
              Asked why no flag
  is studded in his coat lapel
  or decorates his aerial, a veteran
  responds, "I wear my flag
  on my heart—I don't wear
  my heart on my sleeve."

Today
for once we're spared the names
of occupying soldiers shot
or rocketed to fragments in Iraq.
Collateral damage?
                    Two boys,
their mother and both grandparents.
No names for them…
                    Just Arabs.

The first girl in generations,
    you came when the century clicked
    from nines to zeroes to plus one.
Capped on a pallet, you flexed
    your toes and let us count
    your fingernails.
                        We studied you
    as our particular event,
    our small surprise, our bonus.
Months earlier, I prayed
    that you'd be born intact
    and healthy, and you were.
Today I wish you beauty, grace,
    intelligence —the commonplace
    grandfatherly cliches....
                        What
    makes us crave for those
    we love such bounties of perfection?
Life, just life, is never
    miracle enough no matter
    how we try to church ourselves....
Squirming in my arms, you save me
    from my tyranny of dreams
    with nothing but your version of a kiss
    and the sure, blind love of innocence.

Supinely tanning at attention
 on her towel, Lefka's beyond
description.
               The naked breasts
 of lounging women often lounge
 themselves, their shapes reshaping
 differently with every turn.
Not Lefka's.
               Mounding and barely
 pendant, they're peepingly awake.
They match in sepia her swimmer's
 thighs, her sprinter's ankles
 and her navel-centered midriff
 diving to the loins where gold
 triangular lamé protects
 the first and last of privacies.
Her face is all of her
 from eyebrows down to insteps.
Simply by being, she tells us
 that desire's not the same as passion,
 passion but the energy of love,
 and love the silence after ecstasy
 when ecstasy has come and gone.
Like any orchid in its prime,
 she's there to be observed and memorized,
 and so we ogle like the elders.
Watching, we become bewitched.
The more we watch, the more
 we share with France "an enviable
 ease with pleasure."
               Unease
 awaits us, and we know that in advance.
But now who cares?

          The sun's
noon-high.
          The sea seems placid
as a pool.
          And nothing in the sky's
unclouded distance can distract us
from a girl so beautiful she makes
our daily dread of suffering
or violent death seem suddenly
the stuff of fantasy, not fact.

What purpose have they but to rub
   skin dry by being drawn behind
   the back two-handed down
   the showered spine or fluffed
   between the thighs and elsewhere?
Yardgoods lack what towels
   proffer in sheer, plump tuft.
Wadded after use and flung
   in hampers to be washed, they clump
   like the tired laundry of men
   who sweat for a living.
                              Spun dry
   or spreadeagled to the sun,
   they teach us what renewal means.
Touch them when they're stacked or racked,
   and what you're touching is abundance
   in waiting.
                      Imprinted with the names
   of Hilton or the Ritz, they daub
   with equal deft the brows
   of bandits or the breasts of queens.
What else did Pilate reach for
   when he washed his hands of Christ
   before the multitudes?
                                    Even
   when retired to the afterlife of rags,
   they still can buff the grills
   of Chryslers, Fallingwater's windows
   or important shoes.
                              However
   small, it seems they have
   their part to play.

But then,
en route from use to uselessness,
it's no small asset ever
to be always good at something.

Whatever let it be a pleasure
  made it end like anything
  that dies before we think
  it should.
                The aisles of lavender,
  the sea "between the land,"
  the houses cut from rock
  where Yeats lived last, the yachts
  moored hull to hull at anchor,
  and the wind from Africa that's known
  as the *libeccio* are blurred
  like painter's pigments fractioned
  into bits.
                "Everything's the same
  but us," I said, "because
  we've come back once too often."
French television flashed
  a raid by F-16's in Gaza
  followed by a sacrificial bombing
  in Jerusalem.
                The detonated bodies
  sprawled alike.
                "Same intent,"
  I said, "but different weapons."
The prospect made me kick
  aside a core of cardboard
  from a toilet paper roll
  discarded near a dumpster.
                Later
  we paganized ourselves in sun
  and surf—our way of fiddling
  while tomorrow burned.

                    Romeos
roamed the beach, sporting
their scrotal pouches.
                        Women
wore nil but thongs and pubic
patches.
            So many thronged
the waves I thought of mullets
or alewives surging in frenzy....
Three hours east by air,
    oppressor and oppressed were being
    filmed in battles we would watch
    while dining later in Antibes
    or sipping cappuccino by the pool.

The bigger the tomb, the smaller the man.
The weaker the case, the thicker the brief.
The deeper the pain, the older the wound.
The graver the loss, the dryer the tears.

The truer the shot, the slower the aim.
The quicker the kiss, the sweeter the taste.
The viler the crime, the vaguer the guilt.
The louder the price, the cheaper the ring.

The higher the climb, the sheerer the slide.
The steeper the odds, the shrewder the bet.
The rarer the chance, the brasher the risk.
The colder the snow, the greener the spring.

The braver the bull, the wiser the cape.
The shorter the joke, the surer the laugh.
The sadder the tale, the dearer the joy.
The longer the life, the briefer the years.

Prolonged, they slacken into pain
  or sadness in accordance with the law
of apples.
               One apple satisfies.
Two apples cloy.
               Three apples
glut.
       Call it a tug-of-war
between enough and more
than enough, between sufficiency
and greed, between the stay-at-homers
and globe-trotting see-the-worlders.
Like lovers seeking heaven in excess,
  the hopelessly insatiable forget
  how passion sharpens appetites
  that gross indulgence numbs.
Result?
       The haves have not
what all the have-nots have
since much of having is the need
to have.
          Even my dog
knows that—and more than that.
He slumbers in a moon of sunlight,
  scratches his twitches and itches
  in measure, savors every bite
  of grub with equal gratitude
  and stays determinedly in place
  unless what's suddenly exciting
happens.
          Viewing mere change
as threatening, he relishes a few

undoubtable and proven pleasures
to enjoy each day in sequence
and with canine moderation.
They're there for him in waiting,
and he never wears them out.

Nothing symphonic will come of this,
  nothing of consequence, and nothing
  to silence those whose business
  is creating funerals where widows
  in their twenties carry folded flags
  to empty bedrooms.
                    Pronouncers
  and announcers govern from their desks
  while corporals and captains pay
  the price in loss.
             I cite
  the history of Danielle Green.
She basketballed her way from poverty
  to Notre Dame, played guard
  with champions and honed a shot
  she took left-handed just beyond
  the paint and rarely missed.
Later in Iraq a bomb
  exploded near enough to claim
  her shooting hand.
                Others
  lost more, and many lost
  everything that anyone can lose.
Some say that poetry has other
  themes to sing about than that.
If that's the case, what good
  is poetry that shies away from pain
  and amputation?
                What else can make us
  feel, not merely know, that severed
  limbs and lives can never
  be replaced?
            And all for what?

A day will come when nothing
    will matter but the day itself.
No one will care if what's
    predicted in the *Farmers' Almanac*
    comes true or not—or fret
    with crossword puzzles just
    to pass the time—or ask
    why total frankness is acceptable
    in surgery or love or art
    but otherwise considered shameful.
A day will come when even
    the best will not be good
    enough.
            What's seen as quality
    will crumble under scrutiny.
Total frauds will speak as saints
    while torturers receive the eucharist
    in public and be blessed by bishops.
When salt exceeds the price
    of silver, banks will close.
Drivers will spend a month's
    wages for a tank of gas.
Armies will be staffed by foreigners.
Doctors will be paid in promises.
Gravesites will be taxed as real estate
    and levied on the next of kin.
A day will come when no one
    will remember who we were
    or where we lived or how.
Headlines will exaggerate the trivial
    to make the unimportant seem
    important.

History will vary
with historians until the past
recedes and disappears like snow.
False prophets will foretell the worst
and be believed because the dreams
of liars are immune to contradiction.
The world will change from what
it was to what it is although
the earth will keep repeating
its ballet in orbit to remind us
every morning that today's that day.

Just four months into history,
  Sarah speaks in the key of squeaks
  while reaching for her rattle.
                      Nothing
  distracts her but a televised explosion,
  followed by screaming.
                      Her father
  mutes the screen.
                  The screams
  sound louder in silence.
                      Powdered
  by bomb dust, remnants
  of children litter a street
  in Qana.
              Rescuers bundle
  bodies and bits in oriental
  rugs for burial.
                  I turn
  away to gaze at Sarah
  sucking on her rattle.
                      As image
  overlaps with image, bombdust
  seems to whiten her cheeks.
I make a face to see
  if she will laugh.
                  She waits
  until my face becomes my face
  again, then blooms into a grin.
The silence keeps on screaming.

> The cause of all human misery: the inability
> to sit contentedly alone in a room.
> *Blaise Pascal*

Monsieur Pascal, I'm sitting here
   alone in Scranton, Pennsylvania.
Radisson has rented me this room
   with no amenities but lotion,
   towels, bathsoap and a sewing kit.
My family's three hundred miles
   west by southwest.
                    To be frank,
   I'm not content.
                    Though Robert
Louis Stevenson could say
   intelligent men, delayed
   in railroad waiting rooms
   for days without a book, should not
   be bored, I'm bored.
                    Despite
   three books I've brought along
   in case, I'm bored to my toenails.
That puts me on the side
   of human misery and culpable
   stupidity, I guess.
                    But what
   of those who face the bookless
   loneliness of solitary confinement?
Both you and Mister Stevenson
   might say they should be most
   content, but men have lost
   their minds or brained themselves
   to death in such conditions.
Granted, there are exceptions.

Aleksandr Solzhenitsyn scrawled
The Gulag Archipelago on toilet
paper in Siberia.
                    And prisoners
of war have stubbornly survived
cold years of total isolation.
Excepting the exceptions, you
and Mr. Stevenson make sense
but only if our times of solitude
or long delays conclude.
                    After all,
the art of making time irrelevant
by just abandoning ourselves
to life the way that swimmers
float and let the ocean be
their beds is something everyone
should learn.
                    However, the ocean
must stay calm just as the room
you specify must not be locked
or Stevenson's late train arrive
at last.
            If not, we're talking
human misery as unrelieved
as pain itself—we're talking hell.

CAESAREAN

And the Guernsey lowing in its stanchion,
  waiting to be milked, blood
  on the udders, and the farmer grim
  and saying she is only good
  for beef now as he locks a cartridge
  in his rifle and aims it midway
  between the eyes while the cow
  watches and moos, and suddenly
  the shot—and the cow collapsing
  like a creature losing its footing
  on ice, its legs skedaddling
  right and left and under,
  and the farmer bracing to slit
  the gullet with a butcher knife
  and then the belly at the girth,
  his one arm bloody to the elbow
  as he digs for what is due
  to suckle in a day or two,
  and there it comes—a bullcalf
  black and white and unexpectedly
  alive, its meek hooves paired,
  its eyes half-open and its body
  fully formed but feeble in its own
  perfection as it lies almost
  angelic on the crimson straw.

Victors annoy me.
                    They overdo
their victories with too much puffery.
I've more inclined to share
the universal lot of losers,
not out of sympathy but frankly
in the name of candor.
                    Losers
have the look of men and women
in their natural predicament—
patient, sullen, luckless
and determined.
                    Call it the look
of ultimate acceptance.
                    It shows
how unmistakably we sculpt
our truest profile in defeat.
And history agrees.
                    Not every
country haloed its heroes
with laurel.
                    China for centuries
found soldiers deserving
of pity, even in triumph.
Aztecs honored their champions
by sacredly beheading them.
Was this their way to prove
no head could swell if there were
no head there?
                    Or that
the temporary anguish of defeat
was less deplorable than braggadocio?

Or that the once defeated
  could arise triumphant from their chains,
  as history confirms they do,
  to prove that victories are brief?
Some take exception to such views,
  but, as a rule, they're true.

They're spared the fretting and the raging
   that prevent us from surrendering
   at last to sleep, or paging
   through the past, or silencing
   an argument we're always waging
   with ourselves like Hamlet
   in a play we keep re-staging
   differently each time it plays
   to let us dream we're disengaging
   from whatever fate or fear
   awaits us in our aging.

Because the fear of aging
   makes us deal with death
   without a way of disengaging
   or pretending it's a dream,
   we always end by paging
   God to help us help
   ourselves and keep us waging
   our rebellion like an actor near
   the middle of the final staging
   of a play that ends before
   its time and leaves us raging.

> You don't know what you love until you've lost it.
> *Federico Fellini*

1

A man we loved is gone,
   a car he drove belongs
   to someone else, his house
   is up for sale, and we confront
   mortality each time we breathe.
Reduced to tears by memory,
   we learn the lost are always
   with us.
             And so they are
   since love's the legacy of loss
   and loss alone.
                   What's past
   lives on to prove the legacy
   will last.
             But where's the clemency
   in that?
            Without the right
   to bid or pass, we're picked
   to play the merciless poker
   of chance, and the cards, the cards
   keep coming, joker by joker.

2

It's forty days to the day,
   and you're not here.
                        Last night
   I called your number by mistake

and heard your still recorded
message…"You have reached…."
It all came back—intensive
care for days, one doctor
who confirmed the truth, the nurses
tending you as if you were
their brother more than mine.
And all you asked was, "Sam,
help me, for Christ's sake…
I never wanted it to end
this way."
        And nothing else.
The day was the Epiphany, surnamed
Little Christmas.
              Monitors
beside your bed recorded blood
pressure, pulse and every breath.
Before we left for lunch,
we said our hesitant goodbyes.
You slept sedated, but the nurse
assured us you could hear.
The last to speak was Sam,
who carried both our names
as dearest his mother insisted
and whom you loved the most.
"Uncle Robert, we all love you,
but now we're leaving for a bite
to eat, and if you have
to go while we're not here,
it's okay… we'll understand."
He kissed your forehead twice,
then held you in his arms.

Ten seconds later you were gone,
  as if his words had given you
  permission.
            Later he told me
  you parted your eyelids,
  and your eyes were blue, not brown
  as we had known them all your life.
No one could account for that.

  3

Some say the three worst things
  are losing a child, a mate
  or a brother or sister.
                    Some say
  the order's right, some say
  it's wrong, but what's the point?
All losses to the losers stab alike
  because they're all the worst.

  4

You're buried in the same plot
  with our uncle, our cousin, both
  grandparents, our young mother
  and our great aunt who raised us
  when our mother died and made us
  what we were and are.
                    In the end
  it came to family after all.
By intuition or epiphany,
  you picked your gravesite decades
  in advance as if you somehow

knew what none of us
could know.
                    Just weeks before
you died, you said that death
no longer scared you though
you feared it all your life.
Later, we honored your bequests
    and sorted through your papers
    and effects.
                    We learned you were
the same in public as you were
at home—but more so.
                        What else
is there to say except,
"So long for now, dear Bob."
Since brothers are forever brothers,
    you're here and elsewhere all the time
    for me exactly as you are
    and always were—but more so.

For Robert George Hazo

> This seeing the sick endears them to us, us too it endears.
> *Gerard Manley Hopkins*

Named after Swanson the star,
  she knew good actresses from bad
  and did some acting herself.
But that was years before
  the three-pronged cane, the walker
  and the wheeled and cushioned chair.
"Sometimes I could scream," she said,
  "but why, what good would it do?"
Everything declinable declined
  except her will.
               The nurses
were amazed, "We've never cared
for anyone like her."
               Roses
brought her to tears along
with memories of those she loved.
She aimed a special scorn
  at frauds and hypocrites.
               "Some women
marry money, and there's a name
for that...."
           "If being Christian
means forgiving someone
who harmed anyone I loved
and never even apologized,
I think that's asking a lot...."
At eighty-two she hated
  "being trouble for the nurses,"
who already loved her frankness
and her bold contempt of death.

To anyone who came to visit,
   she would smile and say, "Still here."
If dying were a play—and that
   her final line—, she said it
   jauntier than Swanson ever could.
Those selfsame words said something
   surer and beyond denial
   when she died.
                The nurses understood.

> The sight of a naked woman makes me think
> of her skeleton.
> *Gustave Flaubert*

Flaubert can speak for himself.
To me the sight of a naked
  woman overwhelms what passes
  for composure.
                Women, of course,
  would see no more than just
  another of their gender—everything
  the same in general but different
  in specifics.
              Most men would focus
  solely on specifics.
                But where's
  the fault in that?
             I've had
  my fill of puritans who claim
  we're only human from the waist
  up.
    They're always left
  to cope with interruptions from the waist
  down.
      I say we're not
  so halved, that honest passion
  is as civilized as reason
  and that all who mumble their denials
  face frustrations that denial breeds.
I find them cold in moments
  of affection, drawn to violence
  and totally devoid of mirth.

They have the villainies of soldiers
   isolated and removed from all
   refinements that define our happiness?
The regimen's no different for assassins,
   heavyweights preparing for a bout
   and all who scourge their bodies
   in the name of God.
                  Frankly,
   the sins of Casanova pale
   beside the cruelties of chaste
   fanatics hardened by suppression.
Meanwhile the body's blamed
   for what suppression caused....
And yet, indulgers in excess
   seem no less hardened at the end.
St. Augustine of Hippo, Xavier
   and John Donne condemned
   in retrospect the dreams of love
   that women roused in men.
Preparing to be dead, they preached
   renunciation of the flesh in sermons
   brilliant but depressing.
                  Why?
Who finds deliverance in shame?
I own two sculptures that suggest
   the opposite.
             One is the head
of a woman carved from black
marble.
            Her nose is Romanly
bridgeless, her eyes lidded
and her neck like a dancer's arched
as far back as possible.

If she is dreaming, she will dream
    forever.
            The second is a torso
in limestone—headless, armless,
legless.
            From neck to breasts
to hips, what's true of women
everywhere seems even truer
in the shameless nudity of stone.
I have no interest in her skeleton.

Looking back or forward
  never works.
               Distortion
poisons hindsight, and presumption
renders foresight unreliable.
Right now is all that's real,
  and that's just time enough
  to live without revision or analysis.
Deafened and dulled by the dead
  words of the living, I read
  the living words of the dead
  (plus two beyond cajolery)
  for guidance.
               And guidance it is.
Their books are there to be
  consulted when the need
  demands it.
               I learn from them
  what lovers learn from love
  but find impossible to say.
It's like a silence to be shared
  as secrets, gifts or meals
  are shared.
               Otherwise, nothing
  is different.
               The news is bad,
  the market volatile, the weather
  sunny and the traffic heavy.
Cowards are shrewder than heroes
  and long outlive them.
               Talkers
  outnumber doers.

                        One
out of ten of us is marked
for sudden death while all
the other nine will linger.
                        War
and executions qualify as legal
murders, but who shall say so?
Yesterday in consultation with Camus,
I mentioned how absurd it is
to know such facts and not
despair.
                    Camus replied
that consciousness is all—just
consciousness—despite the odds.
This morning I reviewed Pascal
and found his wager with God
a sensible conclusion.
                        Later
I'll visit Richard Wilbur.
                        And tomorrow?
Tomorrow I'll reread a poem
by Szymborska and learn how poetry
can polka even in the midst
of sadness, madness and confusion.

For Jo McDougall

AND THE TIME IS

We have come to the point of decision,
  and the hands of the clock say—be careful.
We've learned from the past that our choices
  are one or the other or neither,
  and the hands of the clock say—be careful.
We have readied ourselves for the challenge
  by weighing the odds and the chances
  of what will result from our choices,
  and the hands of the clock say—be hopeful.

We're not what we were when we started,
  and the hands of the clock say—it's over.
Our yesterdays lengthen like shadows
  that fade when we no longer cast them,
  and the hands of the clock say—it's over.
Despite what it brings to surprise us,
  we treasure each day in its passing
  though we know that we pass as it passes,
  and the hands of the clock say—discover.

We sit on the porch every evening,
  and the hands of the clock say—be watchful.
We study the leaves in their turning
  from green to vermilion to purple,
  and the hands of the clock say—be watchful.
While we stare at the sky in its vastness
  and name every star in the distance,
  we dwindle to scale in the balance,
  and the hands of the clock say—be grateful.

The dead come to life in our dreaming,
  and the hands of the clock say—remember.
The words of a prophet keep haunting
  the ones who ignored him when living,
  and the hands of the clock say—remember.
The world that we think is around us
  is neither before nor behind us
  but always within us, within us,
  and the hands of the clock say—forever.

Michael Simms, Executive Editor

Snow White Horses, Selected Poems 1973–88 by Ed Ochester

The Leaving, New and Selected Poems by Sue Ellen Thompson

Dirt by Jo McDougall

Fire in the Orchard by Gary Margolis

Just Once, New and Previous Poems by Samuel Hazo

The White Calf Kicks by Deborah Slicer ● 2003, selected by Naomi Shihab Nye

The Divine Salt by Peter Blair

The Dark Takes Aim by Julie Suk

Satisfied with Havoc by Jo McDougall

Half Lives by Richard Jackson

Not God After All by Gerald Stern (with drawings by Sheba Sharrow)

Dear Good Naked Morning by Ruth L. Schwartz ● 2004, selected by Alicia Ostriker

A Flight to Elsewhere by Samuel Hazo

Collected Poems by Patricia Dobler

The Autumn House Anthology of Contemporary American Poetry, edited by Sue Ellen Thompson

Déjà Vu Diner by Leonard Gontarek

Lucky Wreck by Ada Limon ● 2005, selected by Jean Valentine

The Golden Hour by Sue Ellen Thompson

Woman in the Painting by Andrea Hollander Budy

Joyful Noise: An Anthology of American Spiritual Poetry, edited by Robert Strong

No Sweeter Fat by Nancy Pagh ● 2006, selected by Tim Seibles

Unreconstructed: Poems Selected and New by Ed Ochester

Rabbis of the Air by Philip Terman

Let It Be a Dark Roux: New and Selected Poems by Sheryl St. Germain

Dixmont by Rick Campbell

The River Is Rising by Patricia Jabbeh Wesley

The Dark Opens by Miriam Levine ● 2007, selected by Mark Doty

My Life as a Doll by Elizabeth Kirschner

The Song of the Horse by Samuel Hazo

● winner of the annual Autumn House Press Poetry Prize

Cover and text design by Kathy Boykowycz
Cover photo by William Albert Allard

Text set in Adobe Garamond, designed in 1989 by Robert Slimbach
Titles set in Trajan, designed in 1989 by Carol Twombly

Printed by Thomson-Shore of Dexter, Michigan,
on Nature's Natural, a 50% recycled paper